Solitary Workwoman

Rochelle Owens is the author of sixteen previous collections of poetry, including *New and Selected Poems 1961-1996* and *Luca: Discourse on Life and Death* (both Junction Press); nineteen plays, collected in *Futz and What Came After* (Random House), *The Karl Marx Play and Others* (E.P. Dutton), *Futz and Who Do You Want Peire Vidal?* (Hawkswell Press and Broadway Play Publishing), and *Plays by Rochelle Owens* (Broadway Play Publishing); the screenplay for *Futz* (United Commonwealth Films; and the novel *Journey to Purity* (Texture Press). She translated Liliane Atlan's *The Passersby* (Henry Holt) and edited *Spontaneous Combustion: Eight New American Plays* (Winter House).

Rochelle Owens

SOLITARY WORKWOMAN

Junction Press
New York
2011

for George

Let him or her who has keen ears of inner understanding pant for these words with a burning love for my image

Hildegard of Bingen

If we imagine the cause of an emotion to be actually present with us, that emotion will be stronger than if we imagined the cause not be present.

Baruch Spinoza

I

Below Ground

This treacherous procession
of words of a HAG
a hag's words are SEVEN
then she tightens
your black silk hood
Her life is among the ELECT
seen in SCENES of
Daily life in a rural
American town
And then the thought
of mundane domesticity
washes over me
I am WASHED in the
thought of the toil of
women women drawing water
And then the thought
of women dragging waterjugs
their MUSCLES contracting
bigger and bigger
muscles like strong woody cores
And then the thought of
a needle a woman THREADING
a needle wetting the tip
of the thread with her
lips trying seven times
her red and pale mouth

as SMALL as an eye
the needle only a blur
the woman's eyes of MYOPIA
crossing over to UTOPIA
And then spitting out
a bit of white thread thread
transformed into wet pulp
the shining needle coming
closer
Such difference between those fixations on
HAGS those you see climbing up the ladder
angelic beings with bloody RAGS of
afterbirth You search always the source
'the fruitful vine' the hind wing of a
flying ant blending the male and female
spheres spawning BLUE larvae
blue larvae into BONES autonomous
bones washed in saltwater
Is knowledge of the hag a search for
something to grasp—thickness of
the fat layer beneath the skin her
enormous bunions a callus tearing
like the hymen of a virgin?

*

And of a hag's embrace it is LONG smooth
and unyielding her winding arms press
her partner's body organs
the CRUSH of her knees will fracture
the spine of a youth who cowers
before her but the hero who lies down
beneath her flattening and pushing
his backbone into the earth like the
roots of a TREE
tensing tensing squeezing squeezing
the muscles of his butt
the hero who lies down beneath her
without sloth or greed and feels LUST
and gazes upwards smiling smiling

with pale and red lips
flickering flickering his long eyelashes
flirting flirting with the hag
singing singing to the hag blowing blowing
kisses singing and blowing kisses
to the GOLDEN belly of the hag
That hero will never creep backwards
on his haunches nor be SORE afraid
he will be redeemed

*

For a long time the hag's skills were thought
to be at the very least efficient
able to do good works
You must HOLD onto this idea like you hold
onto the edge of a CLIFF
your attention slips SINISTER
you step on a nail and draw blood

The good rural housewife is seen making
mustard   she measures closely and tightens
the cap of the jar

Step where you are into the hag's DOMAIN

Isolated   feigning to be BELOW ground
and waiting—her wisdom GERMINATING
becoming active VITAL
She is musing on her version of a
Solitary WORKWOMAN

Suddenly you hear breaking GLASS
your neck twisting to the side FORCE
of escaping a freak accident hit and miss
hit and miss
You begin horsing around with letters
of the names of the hag STRINGLA greek
VETULA latin
You see two gray forms moving towards you

then fusing into ONE hit and miss hit and miss
You repeat the RITUAL   a gray form moving
towards you SPEEDING up swinging and flinging
her gray wool cape her gray wool cape
saturated with piss
The names of the hag STREGA BRUJA HEXE
illuminate gyrating rotating rising upwards
to the ceiling

She is behind me   her elbows winging out
under the FAMOUS piss saturated gray
wool cape
Now she is standing in front of me
And under the cape are a gray donkey's legs
hit and miss hit and miss   a gray donkey's legs
knocking the mustard jar off the table
breaking glass shattering glass
splinters of glass glittering YELLOW
DEADLY women's stuff

*

And of a hag's COUNTING waterjugs it is
a solitary activity during the cold months
light reflecting off GLASS
And then the image of the shape of her
knuckles STYX in my mind   red and pale
hexagonal bumps and stretching your fingers
and cracking your knuckles
you ponder on the degenerating cartilage
the bulbous arthritic knuckles of the hag
You FORCE a grimace ETCHED into your face
like the ancient mask of TRAGEDY feeling
the black letters of the word LOSS
LOSS lashing and scourging your body
All flesh is GRASS
To each her own PLAGUE

*

Practice What You Are

You SAY the words   practice what you are
The good rural housewife
her domestic ROLES the labor of a
SOLITARY workwoman
ripping out the decaying VINES
The good rural housewife lifting lowering
her arms THEN resting she thinks of
the kingdom of PLANTS   rain saturating
the soil   stems   branches   the veins
of a LEAF like the blue and pale veins
splashed on her temples
TEMPLES wherein DWELL the sovereign
crones crones with sack-like abdomens
dressed in full pontifical regalia
And the NAMES of the crones are
Stringla Vetula Strega Bruja Hexe
five mothers in a row
From generation to generation   saying
I'll be in touch GAL

Practice what you are until
EXTINCTION bears down FORCE revelation
MAKE for yourself a mouthful of teeth
like the crones' sharp tusklike incisors

You see her from a different ANGLE
with the hands of a solitary workwoman
filling a bowl with dried fruit

*

Before the end of
the WEEK the first account
of the PERSECUTIONS
of the crones
must be told as testimony
to the concentration
of SITES

15

where CAPTURE or
killing of crones
as the good rural housewife
measures out coffee beans—
took place or takes place
Closer and closer
you PRESS your face
to the rich SOURCE
of grotesque imagery
The anarchy of the BRAIN
in the skull of a crone
the brain that sits
in the skull of a crone
What kind of brain?
Such differences among the crones
and they PLAY their roles
in SCENES of daily life
ABSENT of structure or logic
Except for the logic of
geometric FORMS
the apple is round the bean
is oval
The good rural housewife
in an analytic and hermetic
MOOD pushes to its limits
obscure ACTIONS
and begins carefully
to hoard coffee
She DESIRES to be REBORN

*

If the PATTERNS do not break down
abandon them in spite of cohesion
says the hag—because they are not yours
but the good rural housewife feels
the light RAYS expanding the pupils
of her eyes   And cannot ESCAPE the image
of a NEEDLE   a woman threading a needle
trying and failing six times   And then

the goddess of myopic DEGENERATION
with SIGNS and WONDERS performs a miracle
And on the seventh attempt as STOIC
as a crone about to be set on fire
in a medieval town FLAMES spiraling upwards
the needle only a BLUR   And then
the eye of the needle becoming bigger
and BIGGER obeying the LOGIC
of the elegant symmetry of the UNIVERSE
a celestial SPHERE
becoming a vast HOLE   And the woman's
eyes of myopia crossing over to UTOPIA
The anarchy of the brain in the woman's
SKULL pushed to its limits she feels
WAVES of energy as she inserts first
her head and then her whole BODY
passing like the wet point of a thread
into the eye of the needle
DARK into ABSENT

The chemical energy
in the crone's brainstem becomes
heat light and sound   And the sound
is a VOICE released by the WOOD
and her burning body

*

A SOLITARY workwoman ONE who asks
nothing more from her climate-controlled
DOMAIN than that household tasks be done
And that the DOMAIN wherein dwells
the hag of patterns and sound
in her domain in the hag's domain
LET sound be AMPLIFIED with her breath
her breath forming WORDS

The good rural housewife is COUNTING
jars of mustard while thinking of the hag
'she is a talented vessel of truth'

knowing well that a male parallel
VERSION does not exist

And I see a SOLITARY workwoman
Shoulders hunched forward BEARING
on her back an IMAGE of strangeness
And then the FACE of the hag STYX
in my mind BEHOLD the hag's face
painted on a BRICK wall
her huge LIZARD head and the nasal bone
set between FOUR cheek horns
And I see the words written in LETTERS
of black FIRE
BEHOLD THE HAG'S FACE   And her NAME
is Katalogos for she is the hag
of LISTS of names   And she names
the VITAL organs   Bile duct
Semilunar fold   Anal canal
She measures slowly a SPINAL cord
and feels its hardness

And I see the hag sweeping SHARDS
of glass   splinters splinters of glass
And I see the hag stirring stirring
ILLICIT mixtures   ASH   OIL   WATER
Deadly   women's stuff

In a medieval town GUTTED by fire
the red and pale sun casts a SHADOW
of a donkey and limping beside the animal
is the hag carrying a human FEMUR bone
She is called Helga-Bruja
the donkey woman or simply
SCAPEDONKEY

A hag's words are SEVEN
then she tightens your black silk hood

*

At times you ask nothing more
than to STAND upright
or turn around in a situation
that second by second
surrounds you in a SWARM
of murmuring and terrifying
circumstances
The word STYX slips off
your tongue and like
the intrinsic and extrinsic
CHANGES of a microscopic
structure   like the cracks
and crevices where insects
hide   like the word RIPTIDE
like a solitary workwoman
stumbling on a stone falling
FORWARD falling down DOWN
hard hard on a country
ROAD   breaking her wrist bone
splitting her lip   tearing
ligaments and loosening her
ARTIFICIAL hip
like black black ASH of
September like BULLDOZING
the pillars of AVARICE
like the bony DOME of the hag's
skull wherein sits her brain
like COLDNESS of an autumnal
day infused with light
like the INDIGO seeds
from which she creates blue dye
the indigo seeds that she
arranges in PATTERNS
like her grindstone for making
MEAL
like her skill in making a chair
fitting joints screws dowls
and glue   like calling herself
CLOCKMAKER or simply
BERGEY creator of clocks

like the APLLE of her eye
like the WISDOM of her utterance
of a verse   like vegetal to vegetal
like a CELL multiplying
in your mammalian brain

*

The good rural housewife
is FOUND in thought while
SIFTING out the dried bugs
from a neat pile of MEDICINAL
field herbs   she scrutinizes
the cracks in a blue BOWL
as the NAME Helga-Bruja
CIRCULATES in her blood
she hears the words in her head
        I in my youth strolled
        In a blue wool dress
        I strolled in a circle of blue
The good rural housewife
examines a split open pollen sac
fused with light   she rubs a
bit into her eroded gum tissue
reflecting on the beautiful
Helga-Bruja   she who could
CRISSCROSS her various roles
as wife mother midwife workwoman
REBEL and a clockmaker and master
craftswoman by the name of BERGEY
thus making Helga-Bruja famous for
flexible adaptation in the town
where she was born   And so to guard
her BALANCE she would weed
and worm the soil imposing ORDER
on nature's complexity
She would feel a shape a shape

Of UNDERGROWTH and know
Its pattern and its KINGDOM

*

Slowly and consistently
a SERIES of events
a reality as SOLID as the rigid bar
of a scholar's WORK LAMP was charting
its course

In a medieval town CLOCKMAKER
or simply BERGEY creator of clocks
who was born Helga-Bruja
LINKED her daily life by midwifery
by nursing the sick VISITING
and exchanging MIXTURE recipes

Is it too soon to exploit a female life?

You listen to the question
impossible to ANSWER
You TASTE the word EXPLOIT
its sweetness   letting it melt on
your tongue   While cracking your knuckles
you eat the HEART of the word EXPLOIT
While digging out a SPLINTER squeezing
the thumb hard you remember a poem
about a poet and his bald head
While making the thumb BLEED and running
it under cold water COLD water
splashing HIT and MISS
A phrase   Styx in your mind
          'Any man might do a girl in
           Any man has to   needs to   wants to
           Once in a lifetime   do a girl in'

*

A scholar offers motives
MEANINGS and draws conclusions
to bring her SUBJECT down to earth
wanting to be an ally not an
ENEMY
A subject is assembled   designed
and the IMPACT it makes on us
depends on interpretation
and information

The good rural housewife
wearing a blue dress   her hayre
is the color of BUTTERCUPS
gold and silver sunlight flickering
around her head MINUTES ago
shampooing NOW standing on
the PORCH   bending over   combing
holding a GREEN comb   combing
winding her hayre the color of
BUTTERCUPS   forming the hayre
into a bun   bending over   combing
and observing a COLONY of ants

> Ants will come marching
> one by one until there are none

The good rural housewife stepping
back inside the HOUSE and
STEPPING out again   holding a
canister of ant killer   a canister
of aluminum shining in the SUN
bending over   squatting down
scrutinizing CRACKS and CREVICES
and spraying spraying POISON

Life is marked by RITUALS
and ceremonies   they honor us
and GUARD us against the powers
of RUIN

The story of BERGEY's life
is like beautifully FORMED lettering
A calligraphy A SOLITARY workwoman
positions the rigid bar of the work lamp
ILLUMINATING her version of Bergey
Everyday bears the DATA
Its internal STRUCTURE can fade
And DISAPPEAR in the evolving
TERRAIN

*

Styx In Your Mind

In a medieval town   there lived
a   BAKER and his NAME was Matejka
and his wife called him BUDD
and he called her GLORIA
and their married life flowered
and FRUITED
and the baker's wife bore
two BOYS and one girl
And the girl was called Helga-Bruja
or simply BERGEY

And when the children played
in the garden   the goddess NATURA
created an ILLUMINATED calligraphy
of white star-like BUTTERFLIES
and CASCADES of pale and RED
STRAWBERRY plants
And sweet-smelling and sweet
singing was Bergey

A memory of decaying VINES
STYX in your mind

The TALE of the hags is made
from a TEMPLET
A solitary workwoman must not

falsify the ART of making a
PICTURE of her subject
And truth like GROUT is forced
Into GAPS

And in a RUINSCAPE from
the hallucinations of a banished
victim the WEIGHT of despair
forces REVELATION

What we know of BERGEY is that
she liked FORMS and in an INSTANT
of daily life the SHAPE of an apple
the mouth of a BROKEN waterjug
the GOBS of melting candle wax
were SIGNS and WONDERS

In a medieval town there is a
CHURCH and on the corbel table
FACE to FACE
Is the   POWERFUL hag FLYING over
BERGEY

And the STONE carving STYX
in your mind

Little Bergey holding flowers
her BUTTERCUP hayre wet from RAIN
And pale her arms stretching stretching
towards the hag TENDRILS of her
hayre wet from RAIN feeling coldness
in her jawbone

In a medieval town it is said
that the hag could see the SQUAT of pride
in a creature's HEART

From the INSIDE of a waterjug
BERGEY made a WINDOW
 and CLOSE to her myopic eyes

And moving her head side to side
seeing the POWERFUL hag
laughing vulva pulled WIDE

And looking through her
window the perfect model of a
SPINAL cord
the FORM of the donkey's haunch
painted in ONE brush stroke
by the POWERFUL hag
flying over Bergey

In a medieval town there is a
CHURCH and the ARCH of the CHURCH
is like a donkey's haunch

The good rural housewife thinks—
DECEPTION is appearance
And beginning her DAY sipping juice
She is aware of the ACID
And the RIDGE of her gums wearing away

The good rural housewife splashing
cold water HIT and MISS rinsing
out her mouth while thinking
of her NEIGHBOR whom she cannot
love as herself

There are WILD wandering females

A SOLITARY workwoman listens to the
WORDS and like a warm saltwater gargle
she spits it out
The irritation and discomfort FELT
is a signal

The good rural housewife
her attention slips SINISTER
She thinks of the impacted wisdom

TEETH of the son of an avaricious
neighbor

Sweetness conquers SWEETNESS
So the good rural housewife focuses
her inward GAZE from the impacted
teeth of her neighbor's son
And sees herself as a little girl
eating peanut brittle

There are wild wandering females
their BODIES are truly 'many shaped'
Pale their elbows lifting and lowering

Little Bergey holding FLOWERS
her BUTTERCUP hayre wet from rain
And pale her arms stretching stretching
towards the hag TENDRILS of her
hayre wet from rain and feeling
COLDNESS in her jawbone

The TALE of the hag is
MADE from a TEMPLET and it
exists as a STONE and as particles
of a STONE

And the hag's BODY is 'many shaped'

In a medieval town the hag is called
THE LOATHLY LADY

The good rural housewife carrying
a peacock BLUE insolated tote BAG
keeping BEER cold on HOT summer days
The ice cream won't MELT and frozen
FOOD won't THAW and the milk won't
curdle

'Hast thou not POURED me out like milk
And CURDLED me like cheese?'

The good rural housewife holding
a MAGNIFYING glass   reading
ENLARGED WORDS   moving her LIPS
and nodding her head   reading
PROVERBS

The good rural housewife grasping
the NECK of an ICY bottle of beer
drinking slowly   beginning her LITANY
        Lower than dog shit
while thinking of an AVARICIOUS
neighbor

From the inside of a WATERJUG
Bergey receives REVELATION
And looking through her WINDOW
moving her head side to side
ILLUMINATION

While looking at an OBJECT
Bergey sees it   double   multiply
or DISAPPEAR
by staring HARD she can decapitate
the HEAD of either animal or
HUMAN

And with her eyes of MYOPIA
crossing over to UTOPIA
She is glimpsing PLACE AND SPACE

In a medieval town everyday
BEARS the data SHAPES of waterjugs
A row of wicked CRONES squatting

And from the garden of a
SOLITARY workwoman looking in a
WINDOW of her house
A clock is hanging on a wall
ENLARGED NUMBERS glowing in the dark

At DAYBREAK when the landscape
is STILL
a single waning LINE separating
the BLUE from the gray
When the brain and breath EXPAND
to receive LIGHT and transformation
to receive merit and reward
And to receive KINDNESS and FAVORS

Let VOICE be exalted with a LITANY
Let it be a TREASURE a RIVER of fish
the color of BUTTERCUPS
Let the litany be a WARNING against evil
Against a HIGH HEART   Let it comfort
And CURE

The good rural housewife insulates herself
in the WISDOM of the ORANGE colored
tigerlilies in front of her house

And then the face of AVARICE jawless
and with a sucker MOUTH and wiry legs
comes and SQUATS down beside her
The face of GREED and ENVY
A sucker MOUTH
The face of a neighbor

And the good rural housewife begins her
LITANY
            Lower than dogshit
Lower than dogshit lower than dogshit

TASTE the word ENVY
GAZE at her face   its SHAPE
is a sphere   cone   or cylinder
And like a MAZE
it is a GEOMETRY of Nature
And like the TUBE from mouth
to rectum

Envy RULES and ENDURES
With its HUNGER

Helga-Bruja's KNOWLEDGE
of signs of the zodiac   her use
of AMULETS   ritual magic
conjuring good or evil spirits
And her ILLICIT mixtures
might have been EXTOLLED—

And with her eyes of MYOPIA
crossing over to UTOPIA
Bergey sees COVETOUS-of-eyes

A neighbor VISITS a friend
She LUGS a peacock BLUE insulated
tote BAG INSIDE is a pair of
SCISSORS and a measuring TAPE
wound around her hand

A scholar's MASTERLY command of
sources and the storyteller's craft
like strong TWINE looping around
a BUTTON secures her SUBJECT
And like a HARNESS around
a donkey's NECK and the reins
controlled by a PILGRIM
Empties and replaces PLACE
And SPACE

*

The THREAT of Helga-Bruja
STEMS not from her good works
nor from her behavior nor from her
CUSTOMS

Her EYES like two HANDS
stripping   HUSKS beating dough
WATERING flowers   her eyes

like fingers PULLING back
a child's foreskin

FEAR begins with NERVE fibers
SOLO the PLAGUE spawning

O a young HERO singing
To a DUMB-CUNNING maiden
O maiden won't you HUM
O maiden won't you HUM
Lusting and thrusting into
the CIRCLE of BEING
The BLOOD of the cherry
On his THUMB

'I am for my Beloved   My Beloved
is for me'

And with her eyes of MYOPIA
crossing over to UTOPIA
Her eyes like two HANDS
making double signs of the CROSS
over the UPPER and LOWER worlds

The good rural housewife holding
a bag of FROZEN vegetables
to the swollen SITE above her
left eye   the melting slivers
of ICE exquisite
on her surgical INCISION

And thinking of death and burial
she hears the words in her HEAD
        Take lust with a large
        grain of salt

And gazing at a floral-pattern
melamine BOWL with a seal-tight lid
a cheerful OBJECT   a bridge
between earth and HEAVEN

And inside a PLASTIC pouch are
the CREMAINS of her Beloved
And she WONDERS
If the SPIRITS of the rain wind
SUN snow dirt dust
and bird droppings and MORE
are with her BELOVED

And the good rural housewife
HOLDS out her hands to a LEPER
A leper wanting PROOF
of POWERFUL love WANTING
to vomit into her HANDS
And like ONE who FORESEES
the outcome of her deeds
She BECOMES a vessel
Of powerful LOVE

Her SWEET maiden's face
outlined against PRIDE and WRATH
is visible   the APPLE of HIS eye

> 'All seems infected that
> the infected spy
> As all looks yellow to
> the jaundiced eye'

Drawing ATTENTION to herself
Helga-Bruja is called
VAIN and SLOTHFUL

And swinging and flinging her
gray wool CAPE

And sloth has no definite
FORM and cannot be NAILED or
tied down

And her unlettered WISDOM
and REVOLT

Her use of suction cups and illicit
MIXTURES   the urine from
a she-donkey
And Bergey grinds it all to PULP
        My reeking therapy
        And my source is the she-donkey
And Bergey GRINDS it all to pulp

PRIDE   ENVY   GLUTTONY   WRATH

Until EXTINCTION bears down

The good rural housewife
reflecting on SKILLS of a former
Age while clipping an INGROWN
toenail   the scissors
curving BLADE slipping
SAFELY under a nail

Feeling tranquil TRUSTFUL
and ALERT to her NEED to bless
And wanting BLESSING

Delicately sweeping with crooked
fingers her nail parings
into her palm

The EARTH all a PSALM

Admiring BEAUTY in the FORM
of her antique chair   thinking
of the MASTER craftswoman
and her CREATION of a CHAIR

Seeing her BELOVED sitting
in the antique chair of RICH
Rococo REVIVAL
Knowing that no one else is
ABLE to injure or BENEFIT
or do GOOD or SAVE

her BELOVED from hurt
As a slave in a DUNGEON
As a slave in the master's POWER

'And as the dry heart flows
sweetly with tears tears bitter
and salty'

The good rural housewife TASTING
the tears on her lips
lifting a seal-tight LID
A   FLORAL-PATTERN melamine
BOWL inside a plastic pouch
mingling her nail parings
mingling her BELOVED'S cremains

SPIRITS of the rain wind SUN
snow dirt dust and bird droppings
and MORE are with her BELOVED

*

A scholar having an AGENDA
like a skilled TRADER organizing
wares and goods   packing and piling
efficiently   fitting tightly or
loosely NUTS and BOLTS

A skilled TRADER stacking OBJECTS
in PLACE and SPACE

A medieval town ATTRACTS
ascetics   beggars   cooks   heretics
jugglers   pilgrims   scholars   traders

The red and pale sun casts a SHADOW
of a donkey and leading the animal
is a limping Helga-Bruja
the donkey woman or simply
SCAPEDONKEY

Their quest is irregular   evolving
it is a FAULTLINE

A limping Helga-Bruja with a YELLOW cap
on her bald head
Attached to the yellow cap are
Strange SIGNS SPOTLIGHTS
and the signs number SEVEN

Pale the SKULL of the hag
the skull formed from CORAL reefs
PALE her spine and tailbone
surrounding an island

then she tightens your black silk hood

*

In the THRIFT shop on MAIN Street
Everyday bears the DATA of hope
or a WISH
ENTERING the browser smells fetid
odor of sweat glands hair follicles
and poisonous farts gases of
ICONIC power transformed
And EMBEDDED like tesserae
An old man who BAKES his own bread
who likes snacks of fresh fruit
methodically RAKES through
a BIN finding an orange-stained
wool sweater of a CHILD

A VOICE saying the LATIN root
of sauce is SALT

The good rural housewife
volunteering HOURS of the week
chuckling   seeing a little
CHILD eating spaghetti

ONE strand at a time SMEARING
marinara sauce on her cheek

She says that the sweater is a
VINTAGE item and hand-knit
knowing it is not

The old gent PAYING a thrifty price
Exits wearing a HAPPY-FACE

The good rural housewife
seeing the old gent's decapitated head
attached to a SKATE BOARD

A gift offering from Salome

A sprig of PARSLEY
and an orange tigerlily dangling
from the mouth

It is a gift offering

PALE her elbows winging out
lifting lowering her arms again and again
PALE her elbows winging out

*

DEPARTURE in the morning light
like a blank sheet of paper
or the blind eye of a juggler
exudes THREAT

Arrival demonstrates DOMINION

And with her eyes of MYOPIA
Crossing over to UTOPIA
she is glimpsing PLACE and SPACE

Forgetting her body   preparing her

SOUL Helga-Bruja anoints herself
Neither RITUAL nor good judgment
nor speed of the maned wolf
nor the grimace of a lunatic
THWARTS chaos

The red and pale sun CASTS a shadow
of a donkey led by a limping
Helga-Bruja on her way
to a medieval fair

On the left side of her face
is a CALLIGRAPHY of wart-like scales
A spiritual geometry

Behold SCAPEDONKEY
sitting in the Bishop's CHAIR
wanting REST wanting to sit down
and WASH her feet   wash her feet
with water   clean her infected skin
with water

Outside a WINDOW a Thrift Shop
on Main street   in the HEAT of light
an ARTIFACT pulsates like a vein
GLOWS pale and red
An OBJECT of ritual use

The good rural housewife hears
the SCREEN door open and close

There STANDS a child with
BUTTERCUP hayre

The good rural housewife
clears the counter and sets down
a PLACE MAT a clever
minimalist DESIGN a place mat with
a POCKET an object inside

A voice whispers   an AMULET
of venetian glass and gold leaf
WORN by a noblewoman a noblewoman
who BECAME a saint

Her eyes of MYOPIA crossing over
To UTOPIA

A rash burns a PATH of skin
a HANDWRITING moving up and down
human skin   turns to sludge
And the FEET of the saint
are a CODEX

Lay the AMULET on any PART
Of your CORRUPTION
Let emitting ELEMENTS cure your
affliction   your RANCOR

*

Gain and Loss

From OBJECTS unearthed in a medieval
DUMP a skilled trader makes
a CATALOGUE sees PROFITS in waste
sees SIGNS a good first week of business

Helga-Bruja works BACKWARDS
unlike a skilled trader she wants to
BUILD to build with her hands
a HOLY LADDER

A biblical allusion says a scholar
Place SPACE continuous

A HOLY ladder with SILVER rungs
and on the rungs she will DISPLAY
her WARES diverse objects amulets
bangles CLOCKS dildoes fancy

embroidery gilded hats ink
jews coins knives   Latin letters MEASURE
spoons NEEDLES opium paper
quarrel pitch   rosewater
SALT tape   urine cure   virgin breath
wart cure yellow X zodiac signs

The hands of the juggler TURN and SPIN

Helga-Bruja astute brave SEEKS out
customers nobles persecuted peasants
ALL bedazzled

At a medieval fair OBJECTS are bought   sold
replaced   Banal STUFF like fish hooks
lay in steady supply

Gain and loss are not under man's control

Helga-Bruja wanting to BOOST sales
a supply of fish hooks exhibits samples
on her HOLY ladder calling the wire
FORMED into fish hooks
Saint Peter's wire LUCKY wire
in a CATEGORY of devotional objects
like crosses   mosaics   icons
and illuminated manuscripts
INFUSED with DIVINE presence

Helga-Bruja or simply Bergey CLOCKMAKER
A thousand years back in time
BEHOLD All Holy Woman

Then the grass withers the flowers PALE
the SPINAL cord detaches SKULL
of an old woman white as milk

At a medieval fair come the cheerful
the gloomy the SHUNNED

The loathly lady left alone   desolate
leaning against WALLS walking through
aisles in a WAREHOUSE
The loathly lady AWARE of her stalk-like
legs   long toes NAILS of her fingers and toes
adapted for grasping a hater of WISDOM

A solitary workwoman FILLS in facts
facts TURN and SPIN
gaining MOMEMTUM in SPACE and PLACE

The FORM of her skull is spiked
On her head is attached a copper-colored
wig   a wig SEPARATED into long tails
long tails of varied lengths

The triangular piece of flesh
cunt of the hag shaped in WOOD
Her entire body   a taliswoman

The loathly lady bends her neck
to read a label on a bottle of SWEET
oil   out of her mouth protrudes
her tongue   it hangs like a DRAPE
over her lower lip

There is a CHASM between a PURE
beautiful FACE of either sex
and the carnal SMILE of a hag

When Helga-Bruja OFFERS a prayer
for SAFE journey   she gives a package
of SALT a piece of PAPER her advice
on bee-keeping beer brewing
and LEECHING a wound

If her customer is a nursing mother
she will give a little ELDERBERRY wine
sweet oil for cracked nipples

an embroidered linen and incense
from SPAIN

COLD of a November day you smell wet
heaps of my gray RUINSCAPE

Others come also to stand near Helga-Bruja's
HOLY ladder speaking ONE language only
mooching for body and soul
They sit BEND and walk next to the wares
A convicted whore taps butts with
a myrtle wand begging and tapping
as in a DANCE

No witnesses no photographs no proof
says a scholar

A solitary workwoman FILLS in facts
facts TURN and SPIN gaining MOMENTUM
in PLACE and SPACE
like SEA BIRDS lifting off the WATERS
in little explosions of SPRAY

Opening ten O'clock MORNINGS
the THRIFT shop on Main Street is a
GLOWING streak of LIGHT It is a haven
The good rural housewife is thinking
It is a haven away from wind and snow

Away from WRATH ANGER PRIDE

Deception is appearance

At the counter stands the DAMAGED person
The SEEKING one He stands before her
Cooked and baked in HELL
thinks the good rural housewife
His long bony head TAPERS out of
a paralyzed neck gentle shirring of loose
skin the MUSTARD color of his face

And the beauty of his hands
gripping the SHINING aluminum cane
And if our LIMBS are unable to
carry out our ACTS?

Her heart and throat feel RIPPLES of pity
ripples of pity tickle her upper lip
chin cheek underarms and crotch

SCENES when she in her youth
being a solitary workwoman who desires
life and loves days that she may see GOOD

*

No Witnesses No Photographs No Proof

The RIPPING sound   the loathly lady
knows it well closing her eyes
it comes from her LEFT from where
the timber FRAME is set
The sound of cloth ripped apart
the sound comes from the wood
the STOCKS fixed in position
not far from Bergey's HOLY ladder

And in the wooden FRAME
a female thief without hands
one who squints casts SPELLS
on infants and BANK notes

A scholar says SUSPICION
in this evil hour starts from a dream
about hags

A cheerful looking peasant pokes a HOLE
through the whore's skirt with a knife
ripping it from seam to seam

A peasant dreams about a woman

Abnormally TALL and thin
He dreams about her night after night
abnormally TALL and thin

Near the HOLY ladder two little girls
are playing a GAME of jumping

The female thief's punishment is
amputation of her hands

The woman without hands
her twisted crippled feet EXPOSED
The CROWD's spirit and sense tickled

Business carried on darkness COVERS over

Helga-Bruja gives the woman a sweet
cooling drink

She who offers a SWEET cooling drink
to the sufferer will see the COLORS
of the RIVERS of HEAVEN

At a medieval fair buyers and sellers
little TRUST without mercy pity love

In HEAT of indian summer drinking WATER
Helga-Bruja's gray donkey a THOUSAND years
back in time

No witnesses no photographs no proof

At a medieval fair the hands of the juggler
TURN and SPIN

And the BUYERS appetite pays off
The glutton's too the more the flesh
The more the WORMS on the body
The meat of the body no CHALLENGE
for the SOVEREIGN worms

Only after the woman MOVED her feet
dispute between two traders STOPPED
two traders closing up their STALLS
near the wooden FRAME
and inside a woman
Two traders STARING at the sight

The humiliated filthy woman's feet
making surprising STRIKING CIRCLES
lewd SIGNS GESTURES HOLES
in AIR like a whore makes to customers
BEHOLD the HOLES in AIR

The loathly lady says   I will go
to that PLACE and then RETURN
She wants to CUT the whore's skirt
she wants to cut a piece of cloth
a garment of a CONDEMNED
female saturated saturated
with PAIN
The cloth is fecund FERTILE
with vital SUBSTANCE
streams of COLOR ODOR and TASTE
The whore's skirt the cloth
the cloth from her skirt

Beyond all   LAWS or   STRUCTURES
a pleasing   SAVOR when it's   BURNT

Faces of WONDER SCORN faces of pilgrims
peasants nobles children ascetics
beggars cooks heretics scholars traders

Flexible is the human face able to reveal
a MYRIAD of feelings GNOSIS says a scholar

The crowd moving SWAYING along with
the CIRCLING feet tilting heads side to side
Professing UNITY Suddenly is congealed into
ONE FACE

A RITUAL of bending swaying
stretching arms FORTH nose and mouth
drawing forcing air the blood BODY cells forming
and reforming the SPECTRUM of ONE FACE
And in the wooden frame
a female thief without hands
One who squints and casts SPELLS
on infants and BANK notes

A cheerful peasant attaches BELLS
to her toes   patterns of rhythm rhyme
a medley a FLOURISH and a fandango
Breezes and cooling sweet drinks
POETRY of the crippled whore's feet

BEAMING is the crowd's ONE face

Toes in the air painting forms like fingers
holding a paint brush   as if on paper or
CLOTH like the fingers of a sculptor
modeling CLAY circles rings zodiac SIGNS
kinetic sculpture FORMS in the air
image BEGETS image passes in
PLACE and SPACE

Flexible is the human face able to REVEAL
a MYRIAD of feelings   an accursed look
blissful cancerous DEADLY   elfish gloating
honest innocent jaded keen lamenting
moronic nervy odious playful queer
ribald satisfied temperamental unleashed
vital wicked Xanthippe yellow zealous

At a medieval fair PROPHESY is born
A pilgrim has a VISION
The whore's crippled feet TRANSFORM
into twin fetal SKULLS and floating over

the HEAD of the crowd glittering golden
RINGS

*

The Dryland Plant

Arriving at ten O'clock
the good rural housewife rubs her hurting
knuckles PAIN should be as watery fluid
PAIN should be as watery fluid
released from the body
in a STREAM of piss   Thinking this
she enters the back room of
the Thrift shop on Main Street
Bundles of unassorted OBJECTS clothes
a combined MASS
formations of CHAOS evolving
like storm systems gases feeding
on the SHAME of discarded
goods   no longer good or simply
not GOOD enough

The garments STUFFED into sacks
cloth no longer silky or INTACT defects
exposed or hidden MASKED with tape
stitched together with needle and thread
debased TAINTED with bodily sin
ugly old waiting to be PULLED out cut apart
RECONSTRUCTED

She slips her feet out of CLOGS
drags FORTH a big black plastic garbage sack
she is in CONSTANT dialogue
with the language
of the corporal CLOTH fabric of both
the living and the dead

Jumping on the pile of clothes JUMPING
up and down PRESSING her feet

45

into formlessness jumping on a trampoline
Herself the INSTRUMENT of transformation
from the lowest to the HIGHEST
lifting and lowering her arms

Spread over the floor   an undivided essence
COLOR of forms
She hears beautiful VERSES solo she spins
backward in time 1000 years
And wrapping around her neck a silvery
scarf a MYRIAD of circles   pale BLUE
rings

Neither a poetry pure or a RANCID verse
could be likened to scenes
the STORY of the before and after   darkness
DARKNESS covers over

The anarchy of the brain in the skull
of a CRONE the brain that sits
in the skull of a crone
Keep the anarchy of the brain the brain
in the skull of a crone at BAY

The loathly lady holding scissors
cutting out PIECES of cloth   neat flat
piles to her right on her LEFT
the FECUND side of creation CLUMPS
of substance a MAGNITUDE
of odors DEBRIS embedded in the fibers
beer charcoal dung earth feather
germicide hangman infusion junk
kerosene leather menstrual nicotine
opium pauper quantity of raw
semen threadbare unhallowed vomit
zenith of wax X yucca
LAYERS of mixtures separating
coagulating branching off
tiny clustered chambers pumping

passing blurring lines between
human skin and CLOTH

Arising from her bed each morning
TORN from the HOLE the abyss the night
knowing MEANING is pursuit pursuit
is meaning meaning comes only
while she is WALKING

Rinsing her mouth out AWARE
of the twenty foot tube inside her
aware of its JUSTICE and CAPTIVITY
Alert to danger signals WITHIN
Thinking We are forced to put up
with NATURE
And spitting out antiseptic

The dryland its SUBSTRATUM
vegetal to vegetal
She is dressed in shrimp PINK
is garbed in shrimp pink
garbed in a young girl's frock
at the TOP of her thighs flutters
the HEM of her skirt
Hidden are the dark brown crusts
of skin HIDDEN like cockroaches
from the light

The loathly lady's desire to WALK
in PLACE and SPACE a pilgrim moving
through a crowd a memory of a PICTURE
A pilgrim moving through a crowd

Helga-Bruja clanging BELLS standing
near the Holy Ladder its silver RUNGS display
SUPREME diversity exceptional STUFF
gifts from foreign dignitaries DECAPITATED
aristocrats monks and seers

Helga-Bruja's gray donkey wears
a SANCTIFIED saddle smelling of myrrh
Bergey's creatures are protected from
PLAGUE the laughing mockers say
RIVALS who like to squash   twist and DAMAGE
wares exploiting the frustrated   weary   lonely
customer

The loathly lady wearing ballerina bow
shoes slipping through the spreading MASS
a mass that rolls and SLIDES grips the ground
in PLACE and SPACE

Helga Bruja's clanging bells   Arrival of
NEW remedies illicit mixtures elixirs powdered
boar tusk goose eyes astrological charts Fiji
CLOTH spices and herbs from Egypt cages
of monkeys and pigeons

The loathly lady slides CLOSE raps her knuckles
on a cage   she RATTLES the cage of two DWARF monkeys
dozing on a MAT light brown moths emerge from
the fibers   Pin size holes of soreness enter her
she stands and TILTS her pelvis resting against
the HOLY ladder

At a medieval fair during CARNIVAL
a ROTATION of gamblers   beggars   hustlers
peddlers artists writers
and PICKPOCKETS efficiently working
missing nothing the ultimate aim
YIELDING up money from the churning
crowd

The fingers on the hands of a gifted thief
Bozzi Gripp   like INSTRUMENTS
UNAFRAID of a leper's puke or ANYTHING
driven down in a medieval dump

And in the dust of the feet of the SUFFERER
She will drink pain thirstily

A GOOD theft comes by PLAN and training
CUTTING quickly deftly with a razor
unaffected by HAZARD or fear
A good thief MAKES the money BEAD up
and roll off the victim makes the money
bead up and roll off the victim
like candle wax

Bozzi Gripp has her way of PUSHING
anywhere with EASE and grace

The loathly lady tilting and pressing her
fragile old pelvis bone against the HOLY ladder
aware of her shrimp PINK ensemble
her ballerina bow shoes MAJESTIC before
her audience

The loathly lady watches Bozzi Gripp
Musing—she is an INSTRUMENT that cuts
CLOTH but not human skin musing
the instrument will never DULL wear out
or rust

And the loathly lady sees the MIRACLE
of a good theft BEHOLD
A perfect theft a perfect theft PERFORMED
like a copulation like a PRAYER
The gliding fingers of the thief
SLIPPED a razor into CLOTH cut out
a POCKET the yielding cloth being in
the proper STATE of mind
for its own VIOLATION bore not
a GRUDGE

The loathly lady walking SOLO when I in my youth
worked this profane text

*

Rumors of Flood Plague Fire

A SOLITARY workwoman says
And in a bucolic SETTING a cheerful peasant
and his wife a baby in her arms PART
of the eager crowd

And seeing an INNOCENT gray donkey
gray donkey drinking water
Leg-of-donkey BOUND up in purple cloth
Under is a JAGGED wound
Helga-Bruja's gray donkey standing near
The HOLY ladder

A clump of STRAW sticking out the peasant's shoe
slimy stinking with his sweat and SWEAT could
make the soil to SPROUT
And mother's milk from leaking nipples
SATURATE her blouse
The loathly lady wants EARTHLY treasure
And her hands open and close

Then a RUSH of old women and young girls
gather together at the STOCKS
whispering the name of the victim
It is Barbara Merle the cross dresser
She can swallow leeches eat honey from
a beehive   skitter like a CRAB
and MESMERIZE a monk

The loathly lady with neck HOOKED
hears rumors of FLOOD PLAGUE FIRE
in every PLACE and SPACE

The cheerful peasant mother and child
a blanket the color of MUSTARD a BASKET
filled with bread meat and beer
Later the honest fellow will suck goat's milk
right out of the goat
And make the baby LAUGH

And in a bucolic SETTING a medieval fair
in SPACE and PLACE

At a medieval fair
every buyer carries a SACK wanting
to fill EXCESS turns to waste
And in her house a THRIFTY peasant
snips charred tips of burning candles

A scholar says   A story reflects the world
of the TELLER
A SOLITARY workwoman MUSES
The MOUTH of the corpse keeps opening

In a PUBLIC domain a cross dresser's head
HANGS out the HOLE reduced to a
HEAD of scorn
A SCORNING head becomes
a scorned head ENSHRINED in a wooden
CIRCLE the Laughing Stock is
Barbara Merle

The words slip off your tongue
laughing stock

The HOLY cross dresser surrounding her
a noisy singing and dancing crowd a JOYOUS
kiss-me-twice belching VITAL multitude
addicts bigots cooks derelicts end-time
fucksters good husbands intoxicated jokers
kerchiefs liars munchausen nationalists
oldsters plague questioners

ragamuffins sojourners tattooers
upperclass virgins X wench youth zanies

A hag with a blood-dyed wig
carries a SIGN: Helga-Bruja's curative
spider webs are SATANIC a wound
on the back of her hand a STIGMATA

The cross dresser covers her/his
UNMATCHED self She UNFOLDS her inner
narrow STRIP it is her   essence her REVOLT

DECEPTION is appearance The male garments
are a color and a PERFECT line unbroken

Under a DARKENING sky the cheerful
peasant SQUATS looking at the female
cross dresser her body as small as a child's
Thinking—he could put her in his POCKET
And tilting his head and peering up
the LEFT nostril of the figure in the wooden
FRAME the nostril's twisting PATH
A SPIRAL staircase

And in the father's fingers a SHARD of glass
GREEN bottle glass green bottle glass
INFUSED with light

Like a KALEIDOSCOPE turning slowly

*

Every Day Bears the Data

The cheerful peasant in his HOUSE
early morning frost like cut crystal casts
soft light a spider web SHIMMERS
a silver thread a SILVER thread
in soft light

SOLO she spins a SOLITARY activity
The WEB spun STRETCHED before
And after GENESIS

A spider her PLACE bound by DANGER
Sinister and her WOES begin

And with blood she is strengthened
And with blood she is sustained

The cheerful peasant SHUFFLES his
Thoughts—And the hag's body is 'many shaped'
Great and sharp the teeth the teeth of a
shape-shifting crone

And in his mammalian brain
a SWEET perversity

Two stomachs to EAT and none to work
A STIGMATA on the BACK of her
Hand   like a leech GORGED with blood

FLOOD   FATIGUE   FIRE

And in a RUINSCAPE
from the hallucinations of a banished victim
the weight of despair forces REVELATION

*

A scholar finds what he or she LOOKS for
Close ups a CHANNEL
And connects two EVENTS

A SOLITARY workwoman ponders
A JUGGLER'S art An ALTRUIST'S merit

Near the Laughing Stock   the little
cross dresser   the girl called Barabara Merle
a group of wandering PLAYERS

And ONE among them is named Abel
And in his childhood youth
and manhood people called Abel
Abel the GOOD

And Abel is an ALTRUIST
And TWICE this juggler and twice
this wandering Player
He has seen a bloodthirsty evil-doer
Bloodthirsty to the BONE

TWICE he has WITNESSED a peasant
his legs like PILLARS
dark and thick muscles shift under his
skin a FUCKSTER doing what he is ABLE
To each his own SKILL

Evil ETCHES the flow of the URINE
shuts down

And Abel will HEAR and he will LISTEN
And he will SEE he will SEE my gray RUINSCAPE

Near the HOLY ladder a group of wandering
players they STAND together And ONE is Abel
the GOOD

Once when they DREW lots—
The hands of the juggler turn and spin
And the master juggler becomes their leader

And Abel DESIRES that the TWO tortured
women a prostitute and a cross dresser
Barbara Merle be avenged Both suffered
mutilation—the subcutaneous layer
the fat padding of their butts SCRAPED away
like fat from a goose

And the hag's body is 'many shaped'

The loathly lady saw the butchery
Better to see MUCH and say NOTHING
The loathly lady's desire to WALK away
Blood and GORE A CATEGORY
And thinking—What if I were BLIND
or LAME?

A blind and lame pilgrim moving
through a crowd

And Abel the GOOD Abel the altruist
with nerve and VERVE
spinning turning and whirling over his head
under his armpits and between his knees
juggling PLOTS SCHEMES STRATEGIES

Helga-Bruja watching the donkey drinking
water

When I in my YOUTH worked this
profane text
That which my mouth knows he shall
UTTER

Justice Justice I shall pursue

Before his limbs lose suppleness lose strength
before exhaustion BURSTS inside his soul before
ROTTENNESS before maggots eat him

A hag's words are seven
then she tightens your black silk hood

*

A SOLITARY workwoman CIRCLES
around FACTS finds out what
she SEARCHES for

In SPACE and PLACE
DECEPTION is appearance

The good rural housewife ROLLS her
stockings down a puffy DARK tan CIRCLE
around her ankle bones

Faythless and subversive are her bones
against the JOLTS of life

She grips your hand and tests her strength
Popping into MEMORY
digging out a splinter when she was
the little rural girl

Every day bears the DATA She scrutinizes
her skin

And in her severe and VAGRANT mind

This is my SHEATH dark or subtle hues
chalky yellow blazing shades of gold
red and PALE magenta   bountiful is the bough
foliage and fruit ORANGE green purple
brown blue violet translucent BLACK ridges
strokes creases thin and thick hinges bumps
loops dents corkscrew gouges beds and
layers of COLOR hapless FORM

Out of the HOLE of Baudelaire

IMMORTAL flowers evil TENTACLES

The GODDESS Natura PUSHES aside the angels
—like trees TORN up by the wind

*

LISTEN to the song a language unknown
a language of a CONQUERED land

Entering the Thrift Shop on Main Street
the retired man FEIGNS a halting walk then
cracks a joke   He says—I will take new
STEPS sliding his toes further into
his sandals

In his brain a RHYTHYM a song
a language unknown a LANGUAGE of
a conquered land—
Chocolate cigarettes and money too
butter on my bread from me to you

ENTERING the Thrift Shop the retired
man CONJURES up FIVE powerful symbols
And THREE are in front of him
And TWO are behind him

And they are the Lion   the Thunderbolt
the Cross Zeus and Jesus
And GOODLY qualities PURITY COURAGE
the celestial and terrestrial
They lead him and he follows
To the   BIN of tee shirts the bin for BOYS
and men

And the hag's body is 'many shaped'

He is YOKED to the hindquarters of YOUTH

Unfolding the tee shirts
with RAISED arms   A thin fluid seeps
BLISSFUL the corners of his lips
EXALTED his wrists hands fingers

His sense of TOUCH body heat
BLOOD vessels in the dermis
the glands of his hands and feet
PUMPING sweat
His fingernails slip easily

tickle and slip over under
and inside

He lifts ONE shirt HIGH a dove gray
triple XXX
the words say—SEAL U.S. Navy

He pets a benign tumor on his neck

A SOLITARY workwoman says
Sloth and LUST cut from the same cloth

*

The Gel of Altruism

At a medieval fair a merchant
has a PROFITABLE idea   he will sell
the GEL of Altruism
And all will CRAVE his product
The famous the rich and the poor

A competitor of Helga-Bruja an observer
of her SUCCESS A man with an
affliction TREMORS
His rebellious left arm a FIGHTING cock
renders evil for evil and evil
for NOTHING

Let the GEL of Altruism melt away
your misfortune your bad luck
May it be like butter SPREAD on bread
sanctify and ANOINT
your goodly head THWART the devil
its SWEET smell Thong on FIRE
BUY Altruism gel

DECEPTION is appearance

Like a friar's MASQUERADE his vapid
kindness hides CUNNING and GREED
For he has a WHIPPING boy
A pitiful and despised
beggar boy ill and worn out a self-mutilator
a boy who CLAWS himself The merchant
FLUSHED the child out of a HOLE
And the child CROUCHED before
the merchant a MODEL of goodness

A thieving beggar child BECOME
his whipping boy A model of GOODNESS
And with a nose to smell out a meal
and the NATURE of a dog to smell FEAR
He PULLED the boy out by the hayre
out by the hair the color of BUTTERCUP

In SPACE and PLACE
The merchant sells the gel of ALTRUISM

*

A scholar says—A foreigner visits
a medieval town
A SOLITARY workwoman says—
A foreigner being that and something more

A traveler crosses the seas a STRANGER
His arrival causes wonder DISPUTE
He goes from fair to fair
Let all come to the HOLY Ladder
Meet the clairvoyant from a distant land
Hear the wisdom of a PAGAN
the JAIN man from the east

Hear his prayers from
BURNT books

The eager SPECTATOR sees
a Dark blue plant A ROOT emerging

from the left shoulder of a hefty
peasant   A strange little FORM
like a root with a head and EYES
open and close in the head

And with her eyes of MYOPIA
crossing over to UTOPIA

Helga-Bruja is glimpsing Gautum
the JAIN man
Thinking—his limbless body and BALD
head HATCHED from an egg
laid in water

Deformed from birth
an ALTRUISTIC mother's deathless love
TRANSGRESSED the law and saved
the life of her unfit babe

She hid her damaged SON and fled
WHERE she was born

And in a PLACE and SPACE

She became a JAIN woman
a JAIN woman until she died   Her son
a JAIN man and a CLAIRVOYANT

And he was a HOLY man a philosopher
and he RODE on the BACKS
of ALTRUISTS
On the backs of ALTRUISTS he rode
from Antioch Lebanon Cairo Jerusalem
Armenia Carthage Ethiopia Georgia
Jordan Syria the Mongol East
Byzantium Cyprus Italy
and the WEST

Let all LOVERS of ALTRUISM

come to the HOLY ladder Helga-Bruja's
HOLY ladder

GESTURES of a SOLITARY workwoman
lifting and lowering gray bundles
And gathered around
the CROWD around the dark blue
SWEET and fragrant ROOT
root of a celestial GRAFT the back MUSCLES
of the cheerful peasant

Sweet-smelling the GEL of Altruism

The Jain man swaddled in white linen
Like Jesus the ROOT of Jesse

The loathly lady PART of the crowd
COVETS a piece of white linen
Being neither mistress wife husbandman
lover mother father fisherman skilled trader
friar or mummy in a peat bog
She covets a piece of white linen

And standing GUARD are horsemen
The PRESSING crowd the hundreds of pairs
of legs and HAUNCHES of rich and poor
robust and feeble innocent and guilty
The loathly lady sees
the swindlers and thieves PLUNGING into the crowd
like birds of prey

The HOLY root the Jain man
sermonized and propagandized   Let the spiritual
and symbolic GARDENS yield ALTRUISM
like beans peas and lentils

And he prays for RAIN

Daily work seemed to stop as though
it was the SABBATH

A coughing and wheezing peasant woman
shifts a SWADDLED infant in her arms
Sharp and narrow the FACES
of mother and child

A SOLITARY workwoman says
No meat and potatoes
One's arms around a child
CORPSE in a shroud

The loathly lady thinking—Daily work
seemed to stop

The dry land plant—It's SUBSTRATUM
vegetal to vegetal

*

Crossing Over To Utopia

Like AIR sucked in and out
like VESSELS with oil and wick
giving LIGHT

like donkey drinking WATER
near the HOLY ladder

Like all FORMS reflected BOUNCED
back and BENT
intangible TANGIBLE
like the Bishop's CHAIR overlayed
gold and purple LEATHER
like the dead loose hayre
of prostrating standing KNEELING
worshipers

Like whatever side of the BED one

RISES from like a MEASURE of barley
or a THORN and thistle

The hands of the juggler turn and spin

And with her eyes of myopia crossing over
to UTOPIA
she is glimpsing PLACE and SPACE

A medieval town ATTRACTS
ascetics beggars cooks heretics
jugglers pilgrims scholars traders

And the face of the hag STYX in my mind

*

A scholar says—Let us look at DATA
A thing known a thing assumed

A SOLITARY workwoman says—
A rhythm begins BENDS in a direction

The hands of the juggler turn and spin

In they come NAVIGATING
the Walker INSIDE the screen door
the Thrift Shop on Main Street
The OLDSTERS the woman-of-the-walker
her spouse of forty-five years   a GRANDSON

A three-some UNCHANGED a thousand years
The young boy their EPIC atoms
molecules and CELLS multiplying
in your mammalian brain

Each carries an insulated tote bag
in COLORS red blue yellow
The word—GUTS in reddish brown hues
The woman saying—

We were LURED by the abundant
SUPPLY of OBJECTS

The mystical power of RUMMAGING
through boxes BINS
organizers compartments

The COPIOUS source
Bountiful the STUFF of life

BEHOLD the data of existence
Things of the PHYSICAL world A TROLL
carved from a stump of a TREE

an old iron pulley a strong box
its BUSTED lock reflects a wrathful nature
an AMULET a molded pewter PLATE
of a crone and a DONKEY

FLOOD PLAGUE FIRE
in every PLACE and SPACE

*

During INTERVALS of altruism
as SWEET and luminous as the eyes
of donkey drinking water
The wandering players heralding angels
Singing—GREEN and flowering the oasis
of SUCCOR

 One goes to a PLACE and then RETURNS
charting the course between virtue
and vice

A biblical allusion says a scholar

The wandering players offer
Helga-Bruja's meat and vegetable pies
FREE to poor widows orphans beggars

and the hungry crones and hags
SQUATTING in rows like waterjugs
like moldy RELICS like vessels
with oil and wick FORGIVING light
And joined together by CALAMITY
are Scarcity and Want
Each SWINGS a rope
that APPETITE must devour

Then the EXPLOITERS come
Two stomachs to eat and none to work
Noses to SMELL out any meal
and a maddening ITCH
Cheerful peasants and MUSCLE men
SWATTING away the feeble crones
and hags knocking them down
laughing at their WOODEN legs
their humpbacks the shriveled chins
and hanging lips

Ugly the land where there is
DERISION of the chosen

Then a ROW of crones begin to castigate
and CURSE and soon all the crones
and hags in UNISON
castigate and CURSE in a LOUD voice

Houses   Livestock   Crops and Business

A hag's words are SEVEN
then she tightens your black silk hood

*

An EVENT happens or fails to happen
No witnesses no photographs   no PROOF

Forgotten or UNWANTED it LURKS

around   It is a WHIPPING boy waiting to
be FLUSHED out of a filthy HOLE

The event waits   invisible   it waits
A mutation   a blur a SIGN significant
or trivial as a PUFF
of breath out of your mouth

Make MANIFEST the event
with VIOLENT rigor   pull it out of
PLACE and SPACE

A SOLITARY workwoman says
The whipping boy   his wet and weeping
eyelids cleansed with sweet OIL
His eyelids a melody a harmony RHYTHMS
of fluid water milk bee honey   wine
a thin trickle of tears FLOW

The good rural housewife is counting
JARS of mustard   She thinks—
From some old REMEDY a poultice of
MUSTARD used for impacted teeth
She focuses her gaze her brain
and breath EXPAND

SEVEN jars in a row SHAPES of waterjugs
A row of wicked CRONES squatting

RUMORS like bats in a cave HANG
and cluster together day and night   rumors
EAT and GROW inside the guts
of the persecutors ATTACH themselves
to their lips

Rumors SPAWN
Suspicion ALERT to still SHADOWS
sees a TARGET and grabs it by the throat

PROTECTORS of Houses Livestock Crops
and Business   hasten together

All the WITCHES shall be BURNED
It is a TIME for burning burning
those VESSELS with oil and wick
FORGIVING light

Fix ATTENTION on the cheerful peasant
the skilled trader with NOSES to SMELL out
the PREY—to DETECT and hunt out WITCHES

Your mammalian BRAIN your nose
to smell out the prey

The cheerful peasant RUNS to collect and
SELECT the crones and hags
The skilled trader jeers—They will
not bring the PRICE of raw and dressed
ANIMAL skins

And in the evening before SUPPER
prayers are said about the halt   the lame
And the BLIND

The loathly lady SWITCHES thoughts
switches thoughts of rain or shine COLD air
or warm air   invisible or not

A devil's NIPPLE or the THIRD eye

One with half-skull half-mask

And she remembers 'a mere slip of
a girl' her skin an EXQUISITE cloth   sweet
and fragrant cloth   Then the pigment cells
PEARL white to black   secreting stinking
mucus from the nipples cracks and FISSURES
expanding and contracting
Insatiable the MOUTH of death

Every day bears the DATA
cold AIR or warm air sucked in and out
The time of MAYHEM has come

PLAGUE scratches word DESOLATE

The time of MAYHEM has come
And all the witches shall be burned

The loathly lady DAILY she watches
the crowd killing their cares the PANIC
of the poor the MEEK
The pious throwing stones at the hags
and the crones

And daughters BORNE of witches
and the sons also STAMP with rage
and damn the ACCUSED   And they
show no SIGN of knowing them

And lurking is a whipping BOY
the size of a tree-stump He brags
about the hags that even he a poor orphan
FLOGS
He jumps laughs and MIMES
with vigor the thrashing strokes
of his good master

BEHOLD a whipping boy becomes the MASTER

PLAGUE writes word DESPAIR

And the crowd makes SUPPLICATION
protection against enemies afflictions
And PRAYS for GOODLY things

Sunlight   baths   FRESH air and pure water

Invitations to the royal wedding of
the GODDESS Natura

All the witches shall be burned

The cheerful peasant
PUTS two crones side by side
inside the FRAME with holes for heads
and hands   And he hunches down and lays
his ear on each half-skull   half-mask

A hag's words are SEVEN then she tightens
your black silk hood

FEAR begins with NERVE fibers
SOLO the PLAGUE spawning

STOIC is a crone about to be set on fire
FLAMES spiraling upwards

And with her eyes of MYOPIA
crossing over to UTOPIA

She is glimpsing PLACE and SPACE

Forgetting her body preparing her soul
she ANOINTS herself

And in her severe and VAGRANT mind—
This is my SHEATH blazing shades of gold
red and PALE purple blue violet layers
of COLOR hapless FORM

The chemical energy
in the crone's brainstem becomes
heat light and SOUND   And the sound
is a VOICE released by the WOOD

and her burning body

In a medieval town GUTTED by fire
the red and pale sun casts a SHADOW
of a donkey and limping beside the animal
is the hag   She is called Helga-Bruja

Her quest is irregular   evolving
it is a FAULTLINE

No witnesses no photographs no proof

II

Glossary of Hebrew Words

avodah work
hamidbar barren land, unfit for human habitation, the desert
lashon hora the evil tongue, denoting gossip and slander
omer a measure of grain

Past two-by-fours scratches   word
UTOPIA splintered wood transparent
BLUE larvae   how minute bits
of damage punctuate until
you look behind
dust   acres   wet   heaps
parchment there's more parchment
how minute bits alternate
punctuate   ash   oil   SCOURGE
fingers spreading hour after hour
left-hand writing

Dirt walks in bloodstream   spots
of RED turn into doodles   smell wet heaps
BLUE wool cool GRAY-Green stone
Lucy female surgeon positions
the TRIPTYCH
encapsulating her life   darker
background   attention drawn
to column of archway   black silk hood
pearls & lace WHITE as milk
drawn to The Book of Psalms
DESOLATION dust
                              Cycles core to core
CLOCK TICKS   malt   wine   oats & straw
coal   lead   plumber work   mills & dams
DAYS collecting   how minute cracks
in porcelain   light etches

nucleus   riddles shell   WHITE fear
etches   scorn   curved
a club-footed newborn   detaches
segments of waterjugs BLUE
face to face self spawning
transparent BLUE larvae

Opening waterjugs GRAY bundles
how she scratches word DAY numbering
waterjugs   the method simple
for young women   broken-toothed
contemplating RED spots
rubbing oil into scratches
BROWN RUST magnified in water
rows of BLUE self-spawning
You will stay here an hour or two
observing the WORK of women
here   Lucy in open fields

She can be seen behind the background
1000 years   dwelling of Lucy
in America
force oil on wood   explain the allure
reverse position   your eye glides
past   acres   TRIALS & TRIBULATIONS
here we are like a leaf driven
a foretaste   STRAW & MUD
allure allure   BLOODY foreground
detaches   segments   flooding
mountains   hole   DESTRUCTION

*

Noticing the room doorway   arched
windows   different from traditional
American farmhouse   1000 persons
make up ideal VILLAGE
1000 years   uncaused   syncopated
WATERJUGS   broken-toothed
young women   look behind

SPLINTERED WOOD   brown rust
Lucy says "phases a solitary life"
uncovers triptych   facing images
eyesocket shut   GREEN

*

Is your disease a mind?
to each his own plague   think about
how invisibility yearns to
punctuate your existence
minute bits of damage   signal
her partner
against lighter background
21ˢᵗ century phases   Lucy whispers
a solitary life
tendrils of her hair wet with rain
smell wet heaps BLACK ASH

Plastic bags bulging EYESOCKET
your skill cutting
measurements   acres   numbering
house after house   empty
a PINK sun   fading film reels
Indian summer   heat of a september
day   1000 people   thousand years
features of her face
transparent BLUE
you draw broken-toothed
young women   the background darker

*

There her partners swing
drive NAILS into two-by-fours
pursue young women   tendrils of
her hair   thrusts out hip
practice phrases like "tell me
anything else before the WORST happens"
light spirals   windows alternate

in your fervor   silhouettes merge
with triptych   animate   core to core
force revelation   portrait of
old women tying up GRAY bundles

"Women's stuff"   salvaged waterjugs
you want to choose BLUE waterjugs
but one with long hair pulled
toward the nape   genesis thinks Lucy
she herself will declare
"how hard a woman with such talents
and a HEART magnified in water"
separates   malt   wine   oats
morning wearing BLUE wool
while doing what she is able
when the shutters of triptych open

She looks at a panoramic view
Indian summer   BROWN RUST
like a leaf driven   acres   reins
of a GRAY donkey
you step easily into   inhabit landscapes
past frozen LIGHT weeks of february
three hours   part of the word
UTOPIA blurred
noticing the room   standing
under arched windows
ideology   ideology   SCOURGE

*

ETERNITY drinking out   out
of a cracked glass   he hands Lucy
straw   earth mixed together
straw & mud   when she tells the story
yearns to punctuate your existence
waiting for water to boil
Lucy's dress of BLUE wool merges
with triptych   blocks arched windows
making a praying gesture

hands her straw   coal   lead
plumber work

*

BEFORE and AFTER she tells this
detail   a beginning site absent frag
ments floating above   sexing a SKULL
Lucy female surgeon with head upward
observing how spinal cord seen
from a different angle MENACE
following you   between the mayhem
descends to EARTH
segments of waterjugs pile up
dust   acres   wet heaps
it will be friday tomorrow

Her GRAY wool cape DRAWN
around her shoulders same cloth
same cloth superimposed eyesockets
eyesockets spawning
transparent BLUE larvae
you hold scales in your hands
weighing greasy bones
bones into light bones into
light light
saturates
ash   oil   scourge

*

DECAY   earliest hit and miss
is a favorite SUBJECT still life
racing past BEYOND landscapes
salvaged two-by-fours WHERE
old women lifting lowering DIRT
makes her quota   walks in bloodstream
VISIBLE
swings in semicircle
minute bits of damage

objects crashing DOWN
as it was a bowl thrown

*

SWEEPING splinters   word SLAY   forward
in time you tapped your fingers
traced the half-skull-half mask
rows of repetitive windows
part of the hidden
sketch   more nails driven
bone held in its long
axis   light magnifies
cracks   how in your veins
core to core YELLOW
here her daily life

SEPARATES until before and after
Indian summer   a thousand slivers
visible like BLUE larvae
as if to   slow down   lifting
waterjugs   you are spelling
word UTOPIA the seven maidens
lifting and lowering
beginning plumber work
with neck hooked   look past
two-by-fours   to Scenes from
the Story of

Here is Lucy   like a leaf driven
VEINS SPIDER the eye sockets   nose
mouth & chin   lifting a mirror
reflecting objects   a fossil shell
you hold out   slowing down
a FORETASTE wiping an apple
pale and red   saturated
ups and downs   your shoulders
pulling   how her neck hooked

biting from a different
ANGLE

*

Slowing down   transparent BLUE larvae
lifting lowering   ups and downs of
Indian summer   wrapping
segments of waterjugs   searching
under STONES hearing the shutters
separate   this depiction
of events
an IDEAL village seen
from a different angle
never like this
freak accident

This is where ends 1000 years
she says   DAILY life whose genesis
magnified in water becomes one
drinks out   out of a cracked glass
salvaged what could hold SCALES
in her hands   to one side
the triptych   off the hook
in the lower corners of her mouth
pale and red   laughing
when you tell this detail
a BLOCK of history

SATURATED mouth of waterjug
for the first time held out of
the body   taking refuge here
her partners PULL knives punctuate
practice thrusts   ups and downs
fingers traced   spinal cord
segments indistinguishable
scapegoats
infused with   malt   wine   oats
dirt wedged in shutters
of triptych

They find old women repairing
handles   waterjugs   repairing
BLUE porcelain   numbering fragments
collecting nail   rope   wire
plastic bags   SCAPEGOATS
cutting GREEN rows of repetitive
windows   story of a thousand
years BLOCKS of history
crashing down   losing in last night's
freak accident   transparent spirals
measurements   broken-toothed

If it's tuesday it will be wednesday
tomorrow   Lucy ties up GRAY bundles
wiping away ASH oil   as if
the outer cover were the only thing
which could hold the attention
waiting for WATER to boil
woman hands Lucy straw   under
arched windows tightens her
black silk hood
earth mixed together   striking
two-by-fours

Forced to cutting blocks   straw & mud
wide open jaws of a GRAY donkey
still visible against darker background
thrusts out hip FREAK accident
knocks against waterjugs   splintered
wood   New exhibit   woman   black silk
hood   staring at memorabilia
fading film reels BACK IN TIME
BLUE waterjugs crack   abnormal
gene calculations   dry   wet   shapes
spinal cord

Salvaged   flat tire marks next
morning wednesday
rules for repairing porcelain
reject damaged   handles reins

80

of a GRAY donkey
collecting in automobile
graveyards   broken-toothed
young women   how spots of RED
mass   cutting BLOCKS   ice   rain
uncaused DUST   winding path
you touch dry   wet   heaps

Parchment BLACK PLAGUE
fourth dimension RED burning
mass extinction wedged RED spirals
implosion explosion
but you still pour scrub oily stains
being a cleanliness freak
slender monkeys spill benzene
spreading spots of RED
hour after hour
she looks behind two-by-fours
scratches word FLOWER

She ties up heaps   wet parchment
The Book of Psalms
malt   wine   oats   straw   coal
lead   plumber work   mills & dams
years   DAYS   collecting frag
ments   burdened   acres   barren
core to core   cycles   DESOLATION
clock ticking   dust
spirals   implosion shut off
closed down
revelation is meditated on

*

Beyond cracks about STARKNESS
she etches porcelain   she etches
waterjugs
she could not help observing
stones   seashells   barnacles
RED AND PALE sun

she says a solitary life
glides   glides   face to face
thrusts out hip
balancing waterjugs
flinging her GRAY wool cape

Catching it on a nail
your skill with a SWORD you draw
broken-toothed young women
you say plumber work   allure   allure
etches   etches   transparent
BLUE larvae   numbers salvaged
waterjugs   splashing   you know
how minute bits alternate
dust   acres   wet heaps
like a leaf driven

Here they appear   crossing Styx
in your veins SEVEN MAIDENS carrying
waterjugs   they practice making
a praying gesture   from time
to time   laughing up their sleeves
waiting for WATER to boil
horsing around   two are identical
twins   pouring   wiping away
seven maidens WHITE as milk
cut from the same cloth
making a praying gesture

*

She holds out   cracked glass   failing
to measure   dimensions   that we may wonder
"the vine shall give her fruit"
scratches word DOMINION hearing
seven maidens laughing
horsing around
crossing open fields   racing
in their fervor
but one with long hair pulled

toward the nape   glides past
heat of a september day

Now notice rounded chin   mouth
parting   when she tells story
how she tries not to knock against
waterjugs
horsing around   under a PINK sun
wiping away   earth mixed together
wandering further
you can STEP easily
into landscapes
you find old women collecting
nails   rope   wire

Here and there   young women under
arched windows   as if it was
a bowl thrown   how minute cracks
in porcelain   ice   rock
DARKNESS covers over
mouth & chin   hands held
PARCHMENT
you practice forming clay
with blindfold eyes
hour after hour   force
revelation

*

When you tell story of the BEFORE
AND AFTER yields bone by bone
she wipes away DIRT
handles damaged objects   crashing down
now this fluke of history BOWLED over
Lucy wandering further BEYOND nudity
EDEN makes her quota
magnified in water
ups and downs of arms WHITE as milk
seven maidens   following
DARKNESS covers over

This CLUSTER moves back
The Psalms of the Book   flashing
under RED AND PALE SUN   her skill
toiling in open fields   seven maidens
make their quota pulling
plastic bags   data on the
SKULL
shutters of triptych close
behind her ALEPH BETH
whispers   here we are
like a leaf driven

FERMENT beginning
a sequence backfires until STRIKING
the outer cover Lucy's hearing
objects crashing down   bowled over
the cracks in clay   that PART
of daily life LEPROUS
the other part cut from a different
angle   forced wide open jaws
eyesockets   HANG DOG
look past the mayhem   back to back
WITNESS half skull-half mask

*

Who has a MINUTE has
a thousand years
the skeleton made up PARTS
until   dragging two-by-fours
drawing   this fluke of   a skull
MINERAL   thinks Lucy   its hardness
detaches   this obscure action
repetitive   You are seeing seven
maidens
their arms floating above
RED & PALE

DETACHES handles a bowl you hold
here the outline oval EYESOCKETS

traced broken-toothed
young women moving towards you
she has a minute Lucy says
HIT & MISS she is
making mustard tightens
the cap of the jar wiping
mouth & chin PULVERIZE
segments of waterjugs
you are where you step

MEETING here little by little
falling between the cracks outline
ESCAPE is meditated on pursuit
of seven maidens REFUGE
from a first step
where young women visible
under arched windows MAGNIFIED
cold slivers of porcelain
how minute bits
alternate your woes DAILY
she positions the triptych

*

BEFORE and AFTER she tells this
detail a beginning site absent frag
ments floating above sexing a skull
Lucy female surgeon with head upward
observing how spinal cord seen
from a different angle MENACE
following you between the mayhem
descends to EARTH
segments of waterjugs pile up
dust acres wet heaps
it will be friday tomorrow

Her GRAY wool cape DRAWN
around her shoulders same cloth
same cloth superimposed eyesockets
eyesockets spawning

transparent BLUE larvae
you hold scales in your hands
weighing greasy bones
bones into light bones into
light light
saturates
ash   oil   scourge

DECAY earliest hit and miss
is a favorite SUBJECT still life
racing past BEYOND landscapes
salvaged two-by-fours WHERE
old women lifting lowering DIRT
makes her quota   walks in bloodstream
VISIBLE
swings in semicircle
minute bits of damage
objects crashing DOWN
as if it was a bowl thrown

*

SWEEPING splinters   word SLAY forward
in time you tapped your fingers
traced the half skull-half mask
rows of repetitive windows
part of the hidden
sketch   more nails driven
bone held in its long
axis   light magnifies
cracks   how in your veins
core to core YELLOW
here her daily life

SEPARATES until before and after
Indian summer   a thousand slivers
visible like BLUE larvae
as if to   slow down   lifting
waterjugs   you are spelling
word UTOPIA the seven maidens

lifting and lowering
beginning plumber work
with neck hooked   look past
two-by-fours   to Scenes from
the Story of

Here is Lucy   like a leaf driven
VEINS SPIDER the eye sockets   nose
mouth & chin   lifting a mirror
reflecting objects   a fossil shell
you hold out   slowing down
a FORETASTE   wiping an apple
pale and red   saturated
ups and downs   your shoulders
pulling   how her neck hooked
biting from a different
ANGLE

*

Hearing word UTOPIA continuous
a thousand years   yellow reflections
splinter   morning to evening
you are able to trace   a bowl
the farthest one   seeing   it from
a different angle SEARCH for
something to grasp   around
your shoulders   you should scratch
again   word UTOPIA
how holding a bowl of water
you raise your hands

In your line   you say plumber work
around a SOLITARY spinal cord
life still MAKES UP weeks of February
all morning to evening
Lucy is here   like a leaf driven
once she gets going   sleeves
of seven maidens   alternate
at last glance   lines segment

ONE is searching   wandering further
dress of blue wool   past
frozen light

A sort of physical TRIP TIK
bringing with it this
fluke of three   hope   envy   charity
alternate VICES   VIRTUES
she positions the TRIPTYCH
wiping away   dust   minute bits
alternate this foreknowledge
hardly matters   exodus thinks Lucy
taking refuge here   with neck hooked
you lift two-by-fours
smelling benzene

*

Peering at BROWN DUST mayhem seen
in her QUEST you could always
practice phrases like "tell me how
did that happen?"
slowing 1000   Indian
summers   your life is
FORCING oil on wood   smelling
benzene   slowing down
this scene playing out   fading
film reels   forwards backwards
seven maidens GLIDE across

The one farthest WAY out   there
look at how her dress
of BLUE wool   swings   swings
in semicircle   STEALS
your attention   scanning
OBJECTS infused with   ash   oil
from morning to evening this
perception   self-spawning
how in your skill DAWN

into LIGHT red and pale
against the grain

SCARCE that you have all
salvaged   rows of NAILS   there
the features of your face
seen   the oval outline drawn
half skull-half mask   narrow
closed shutters   hands driving
nails into two-by-fours
pulling   neck hooked
tightening   one side   WHERE
you close a shutter
it will be monday tomorrow

*

There with   territory   here
mills & dams   WRATH   from time to
time   easily she fills   waterjugs
curved these letters   R
liquid caught   in her hands
making a praying gesture
this ideal village
between the mayhem   an ending
is   this fluke of   a SKULL
found   see her position
two-by-fours

You shivering   angling body
aging   moving these LETTERS
turning a bend   about to ask   can
we   stilling a voice   kicking
our legs NIGHT & DAY dragging
waterjugs   bending body
running before   how her dress
swinging   semicircles   raising
blocking our view   1000
years   in open fields   passing
daily life

Vast FOUND your questions you
ask   rules for repairing porcelain
despite   not answering   what
you are doing   SCRUTINIZE what was
past   two words ALLURE ALLURE
should he wait under
arched windows ABSENT with neck
mouth & chin   in her fervor
how you try not to knock
against waterjugs
STRIKING this foreknowledge

*

Holding on   the edge   your attention
slips   SINISTER   acres under your feet
daily you say   it's neither
HIT or MISS neither HOT or COLD
alternate DAYS what happens between
here & there   she measures
closely   waterjugs
she must glide   her fingers
past   the edge   near where ash
infused with light
she closes shutters

Yes MATTER your hands magnifying
in water   holding on   edging nearing
seven maidens   gliding past
horsing around   light light
scarcely she makes her quota
plumber work HOT or COLD
darkening streaks   beginning
territory   marking   sweeping
pulling   tightening her
black silk hood
her shoulders alternating

Reaching upwards   noticing
how much you can TELL where

in America   ideal villages there
you once dwelled   in the north country
what makes this WOMAN here
gazing upwards at charcoal cliffs
her black silk hood detaches
descends to EARTH
core to core   animates   here
she ties up heaps
makes her QUOTA

Played out   daily   you tighten
REINS of a gray donkey   one side
BREAKS from behind   rope   wire
this scene playing out   larger
yes DOUBT how   before and after
TERRITORY beginning
from a different angles   broken
BURNED into
word UTOPIA
WHERE you are BEHOLD
the TRIPTYCH

Never the TRIPTYCH'S wood
still marked   that part   is
saturated   this racing PAST NOW
under your feet back into HEAT
of a september day
you step on a nail BLOOD
drawn   darker slivers
how minute bits of DAMAGE
punctuate your existence
this is where   begins
a thousand years

Another shutter opens   face
to face   you distance   1000
years   alternate glass shards
VOLCANIC ash   hour after hour
spreading   heat of the TRIPTYCH
Lucy seen making MUSTARD

she measures   closely YELLOW
her   taste   smell   skill
oil on her mouth & chin
splashing   wiping away
she SATURATES

She walks BREATH welling HEART
floating   against the rules her
SKILL with a sword
warring the loss   you see her
with head raised   moving
towards you   meeting here
translucent skull found
she questions   scrutinizes
cranial BONES
how LONG
darkness covers over

Your NAME circulates   all of
a SUDDEN under lightness what
outsider begins speeding up
her gray wool cape   flinging
horsing AROUND it is a bowl
crashing down   when her wool cape
swinging   how before and after
racing past   cracks in
the bowl   ash   oil   scourge
she tightens
the cap of the jar

Since MIDNIGHT how long her gray
wool cape beyond   dust   acres
wet heaps   PAST water magnifying
the bowl   hands of Lucy
loosening reins   a gray donkey
kicking its legs   all your
life   crossing flat tire marks
side of triptych
FLUKE of three SCENES where

you close a shutter
burning fourth dimension

You would FORCE your eyes
hour after hour   all the landmarks
alternate SUSPICION my nights
near where you close a shutter
nothing spilling   only
a bowl of WATER falls
raising questions RULES for
repairing porcelain
who should tell   this
TALE of a changing
Landscape

*

Lighter letters flattened
parts   a solitary life   la disparition
your days drawing RED HEARTS racing
past ASH SCOURGE   all your
shoulders   superimposed MAGNIFIED
in water   KYLIX where its hardness
 curved like a   question mark
a space visible   BLUE larvae
spawning
DARK into ABSENT hit & miss
tipping the bowl

This waterscape FIXED crosses
your mind PAST spinal cord   still
the trunk and branches reverse position
splintered wood   flattened LETTERS
linking parts DARKNESS LIGHTNESS
speeding up
dazzle YELLOW she holds out
cracked glass circles water
splashing Lucy's dress
she must raise her hands
hands her   the TRIPTYCH

So that they FOLD like doors
flanked   name genesis   thinks Lucy
standing in the middle
you answer her   glancing   towards
blurred drawn lines SCENES
become   streaks saturated
triptych   this detail
lighter in beginning   red
PITFALLS points out
scenes GEOGRAPHIC one can
say that your answer

*

Makes DETAILS stills weeks of
February sees GREEN gutted
HOPE ENVY CHARITY in front
of a word   molded by water
A fossil shell found   with
cold slivers ANIMATES
as if to speed up old women
collecting segments   of waterjugs
see them position without
a false motion   hunching
their shoulders

Destroying word SLAY directions
you want to take   when   back to
back drawing segments   of windows
cutting blocks   hardness SHELL
molded by water   blue larvae
spawning   in their FERVOR
over NUMBERS you see them
drawn to side of DAY
daily you position   wet heaps
fluke of three VICES
hope   envy   charity

STRANGE meeting here
where old women listening   she is

telling a story   continuing what you are
DOING hunching your shoulders
pulling   how your neck
reflecting in a mirror   eye sockets
nose   mouth & chin   here is
where   its hardness detaching
forcing the cap of the jar
as if its cracking in her hands
punctuating hit & miss

*

WHERE the only other event
is here NATURE blurred red
RAIN hit & miss all those parts
reflecting what you are EARLY
winter magnified
the features of your face
CORE to CORE   eradicated
from a different angle UTOPIA
remnants under her feet
all morning to evening
again   word GUTTED

And yet what she IS
linking together   infused with
malt   wine   oats   biding her
TIME   keeping one or two NAILS
salvaged repetitive   where
YELLOW segments   bones   light
lightly in time   tapping
your fingers DOWN your mouth
& chin wiping away oil
her rounded chin RED AND PALE
the apple of your eye

I   in my youth   strolled until   cracks
foreground   hem   my GRAY dress swings
in semicircle   light arching liquid
darkening STREAKS   here is Lucy

she measures all morning
to evening   with head lowered
I answer   scrutinize the bowl
background SCENES dazzle speeding
YELLOW
absence of seven maidens ALTERNATE
spinal cord MAGNIFIED

*

No one SPOKE to her   like her
of the color YELLOW   each to
his own REVELATION   boiled BLUE
wool LUCY is in FOREGROUND
lifting her head LIQUID infused
with SPREADING a thousand
years DOWN the cap
of the JAR   falling   she
alternates SEGMENTS   KYLIX
spilling a bowl of water
blue wool SEPARATES

In this BACKGROUND one knows
reflecting how HOURS mass numbering
a thousand years FORCE the cap
of the jar DOWN ABEL to CAIN
thinks Lucy SIGNAL your
partner   but one with
long hayre pulled GLIDES past
moves back   descends to EARTH
her gray wool cape
COVERS over SCENES
beyond RED AND PALE sun

Spilling a bowl of water
blue wool SEPARATES one
in this BACKGROUND one knows
reflecting   how HOURS mass numbering
a thousand years FORCE the cap
of the jar DOWN ABEL to CAIN

thinks Lucy SIGNAL your
partner but one with
long hayre pulled GLIDES past
Moves back   descends to EARTH
her gray wool cape   Covers over

*

Long hayre angles   down her neck
her neck bones linking
MAGNIFIED it is then that
your partner   Lucy thinks
glides glides FACE to FACE evening
evening to morning SCENES
from this tale   1000 years   certitude
gutted SKULL
GUTTED loss begins   translucent
blue larvae racing past
DUST ACRES

Shallow side of a bowl SPILLING
malt   wine   oats   her chin
rounded RED AND PALE
with her head raising LONG
hayre angles down her
down her dress of BLUE WOOL
raising her hands opening
opening shutters of triptych
SPEEDING up this TALE
scratches word SCOURGE
animates CORE to CORE

Under NUMBERS "he shall come up
like a lion" beyond
red and pale sun GOLD VERSES
gutted   slowing down   automobile
graveyards ASH OIL WATER
where fading film reels
slowing 1000 Indian summers
alternating   and seven maidens

from the same angle
scrutinize CRACKS
in waterjugs

*

Face of an old woman CAST
me not off in the TIME of
old age when my
strength FAYLS forsake me
NOT and under water
angles a SKULL detail from
this scene playing out R
bending body TURNING
towards you   where SCENES
superimposed ABSENT
in this foreground

MID matter   minutes matter
in the margins   old women
scratch left-hand
writing DESOLATION numbering
waterjugs   "women's stuff"
past UTOPIA past SCOURGE
21st century DISPERSED
seven maidens crossing Styx
cut from the same cloth
wearing pearls and lace
wandering further

Then FEAR will fall upon
her   back in time   under
the black silk hood   narrow
half-mask   there your
attention   played
played in a changing
LANDSCAPE
gutted TURNING towards
FACE of an old woman

gazing upwards
she walks in ACRES

*

Consumed by FIRE
seized the trunk and branches
Curved DARK into
ruby red   measure your
solitary LIFE
how the background
SEPARATES shutters of
triptych
open/shut   so that SIGNS
and WONDERS speeding
up   cover over

Metamorphoses   you are able
looking PAST your version slowing
tearing the cloth   etching
LIGHT in the north country
red and pale SUN devouring
SLOTH LUST alternating
Lucy's life   like a leaf driven
evening to morning
SPILLING
malt   wine   oats
spawning BLUE larvae

R R you will write VERSES
include minute matters   customs
of daily life   always   slowing
down   when you TELL
this detail   waiting for
WATER to boil   peering
closely WATERJUGS
she measures   slowly
SPINAL CORD its hardness

curved   parts linking
a thousand years

*

BARREN a desert   measures
dispersed PIECES caressed
what are SACRED VERSES
seven maidens GLIDE across
the one farthest   slowing
up   swinging semicircles
ALLURE ALLURE
scattered pieces of asphalt
you close a shutter
ABSENT into DARK

PLUMMETING where revelations
rosettes   red and pale
the one closest   speeding up
steals away   this DESERT
where the only other event
is here DOWN
your mouth & chin   wiping
away oil CAIN to ABEL
superimposed   half-skull
half-mask
VEGETAL TO VEGETAL

Showing them   all the
BACKGROUND 1000 years here we
are like a leaf driven
this is where begins a thousand
years WHERE you practice forming
CLAY handling a bowl tracing
the oval outline   being
a landscape   seeing that
this detail is told
desiring to part DARK
into ABSENT

Offerings   made by FIRE we
are there to tell
SCENES FREEZE of a November
DAY and EVENING
latest miss and hit
as if it was a bowl thrown
over a LONG line
Lucy measures   closely
cracks in the bowl   you see
her with neck hooked like
a question MARK

And before I had done speaking
BEHOLD under
red and pale sun   wandering
further   spilling water
with your head raising LONG
your attention turning
"Women's stuff"
and standing near face to face
are BLUE waterjugs
lifting and lowering
BLUE waterjugs

Wrapping around her head
she must RAISE   her hands tying
under her rounded chin POURING
upon her   ash   oil   streaks
saturated   honey gold
ruby red   peacock blue
ILLUMINATION gutted TORMENT
Lucy thinks   a sheet   of gold
PROSTRATE she must MARK
the end of VERSES geometric
VEGETAL to VEGETAL

Lighter letters WHITE INK
pouring verses organized four
forms right to left SKULL
vegetal to vegetal

GOLD VERSES prostrate
your ATTENTION spreads
ASH OIL WATER
elements   your eyes measure
blue wool   geometric
mark the SAVED
core to core

*

Caressed   mouth & chin
lightly in time RED AND PALE
infinite   her attention organizes
an inscription lighter letters
AMULET to one side
touched SEGMENTS gold verses
IMPLOSION is meditated on
ash   oil   water
magnifying cranial bones
so that they FOLD like doors
open/shut

Rooted   more repetitive letters
spelling SCENES from the STORY
speeding up HEAT ASH OIL
water   caught
in your hands   see her position
waterjugs   makes her quota
BEHOLD IMPLOSION
force your answer
GUTTED red and pale sun
No one spills a bowl
her eyes measure GOLD VERSES

Embedded SECRET INRI
you will behold SCORN no eyes
answer her narrative   verses
erased   a faraway land
under heat of a september day
here are ups and downs

half-skull half-mask
gazing downwards BURNED
into word UTOPIA
gold verses   detaching
COVERS over

*

RUB OIL against the grain
measure the objects blocking
your view
1000 years   customs of daily life
speeding up SIX POINT YELLOW
segments   two nails
piercing hit & miss   She
in her youth thinks Lucy
opening shutters of triptych
Lucy thinks of
automobile graveyards

Edge of VENGEANCE
wood the colors pale and red
this first glance   tomorrow
monday beginning FROZEN
into word TREE the trunk
and branches reverse
position DARK into ABSENT
can you say that your
answer matters MINUTE
by MINUTE
blue larvae racing past

Torn into WORD stretch
melting ice   wisdom of wood
for their TONGUES
are polished wood   seven maidens
gilded and silvered   racing past
BAGHDAD their EYES
full of dust
for all the gold in their

presence is just sand
FAT for a BURNT
Gift

*

Silvered and gilded
REVELATION washing the word
morning to evening   a bowl
of peacock blue   spilling
VERSES ruby red
honey gold   half-moon
shape of letters   rivers
of colors   translucent
 a bowl of water
held out to Lucy   how her
dress of BLUE wool swings

From a LONG line desiring
to part DARK into ABSENT
ABSENT being
a waterscape   while doing
customs of DAILY life
where your mouth & chin
SUPERIMPOSED
in this background geometric
elements ALTERNATE
answers   listening
to her fingers tapping

DESIRE wooden homes
surrounded   together   linked
all those parts geometric
MARKS written
with WHITE INK desiring
to join both   answering
questions by saying
"I in my youth   strolled
all morning"

wrapping around my shoulders
my gray wool cape

*

To be alternating   evening
segments of waterjugs   filling
plastic bags FACE all DECAY
core to core
PARCHMENT wiping mouth & chin
ash   oil   scourge
SWEEPING splinters FROZEN LIGHT
Nothing is broken   seeing
segments under my feet
evening to morning
TELL this detail

Slowly   you LEFT the city
following behind
I am tying up heaps making
my QUOTA gutted   foreground
this DESERT found CHASTISE
against DECAY here she
ties up heaps   counts
SIGNS and WONDERS
alternating words   sloth/lust
brazen/will
and your WOES begin

CHARITY saves from death
Can you scrutinize   this DETAIL
so that SIGNS
and WONDERS alternate
red and pale rosettes
vegetal to vegetal
RIVERS of letters white as
white as milk
she SAVES from death

HOPE ENVY CHARITY
Lucy is in foreground

*

And all because   when you
TELL story beginning
that PART leprous
you could scratch again
WORD utopia
who is SEEN in their quest
this   life is FORCING
oil on WOOD
she must glide her fingers
so that they make
streaks

Paying a workwoman's
WAGES it will be friday tomorrow
on that DAY you shall pay her
as objects VISIBLE
from a different ANGLE
superimpose FAULT
as if on that day a loss
of a GRAY donkey
you are WANDERING further
you practice forming
clay that PART of daily life

Because this CITY was
a great city   under RED
AND PALE SUN
step where you are
with head DOWNWARD where
old women lifting lowering
DIRT pulling with
neck hooked SWEEPING splinters
ACRES of automobile

graveyards   she is the STRANGER
that walked among them

*

SEE when the shutters
open POSSESS parchment
it was earth mixed together
how forming CLAY
with blindfold eyes   as if
she is purchasing
a service SPEEDING up
slowing down
 my attention scanning morning
 to evening
DAWN into LIGHT

STRANGER you are wandering
further UNKNOWN word
scratched on two-by-fours
CRACKS punctuate
half-moon   a same angle
seen   an ideal VILLAGE
wooden homes   Scenes from
the Story of when
"I in my youth   strolled
all morning"
it will be friday tomorrow

Which DAUGHTER makes
her quota   the seven maidens
following   closer   known
BONES yellow
rows of NAILS driven
lengths of wood   absorbing
DAWN into LIGHT
position at the same angle
a SKULL in OPEN fields

she once dwelled
in the north country

*

What does GAIN in knowledge?
how holding a bowl of water
where SCENES
are missing STOLEN
"women's stuff" thinks Lucy
stranger to The Book of Psalms
does holding a
BURNT gift BEHOLD ash   oil
oldest hit and miss
REVELATION where the only
other EVENT is here

As rivers SURGING forcing
a split/Sea of Reeds
desiring to PART
that REVELATION as when
seeing   a great
city   under red and pale
sun   because this city
was from SCENES from
the STORY of when
"I in my youth   strolled
all morning"

Forcing that REVELATION
when the morning sun
seems like WHITE hands   shimmering
how her   mouth & chin
visible   under COLUMN of
archway   seeing it from
a different angle
then her half-mask consumed
by FIRE curved DARK

into ruby red   then FEAR
will fall upon her

*

A bowl held out to Lucy and you
alternate VIRTUES
three virtues alternate
she raises her right hand
touching ROWS of repetitive
windows   whispers
CHARITY FAITH HOPE
separates malt wine oats
how her dress of BLUE
 wool swings   swings in semicircle
here is the only other event

Choose   the direction RETURN
naked   gazing upwards
here cliffs infused with light
shivering ABSENT two words
alternate ash oil spreading
BEYOND racing past
WHERE between the mayhem
mayhem was never like this
you whisper SCENES
from the STORY
BEHOLD SCOURGE

That only ONE of seven maidens
makes her quota
she whispers under RED AND PALE
sun   it will be sunday
tomorrow
Again and again MEASURING
cracks in CLAY blue of
light   in the north country
wasting   a bowl   of water
splashing hit & miss
covers over SCENES

FORM of ruin   cooking pot
thinks Lucy   here are KITCHEN
things "women's stuff"
handling a BOWL tracing
an inscription   verses embedded
here near ACRES ash oil
when the evening sun DARK
into ruby red STREAKS
behind COLUMN of archway
Then she ties up heaps filling
filling   plastic bags

You are looking   following
the WAY that hearing
about SCARCITY
weakens the grip   seven maidens
white as milk LIFTING and
LOWERING all that's left
of this FLUKE
of your story   might be
a SIGN a BURNT sacrifice
the shape of a   skull
DRAWN in   sand

That is all ABOUT scarcity
BE white as milk
Lucy says   in your STORY what
is left   a vat of   ash   oil   scourge
her feet CROSS this waterscape
a split/Sea   seeing that
WHEN with her RAISED
right foot   how her dress
of BLUE wool swings   swings
in semicircle   laughing up
her sleeve   from time to time

Block the other part   a VAT
spilling arching liquid
beyond your feet   from time to time
with every STEP crossing this

landscape   what STORY
is playing OUT in a changing
landscape   into BLUE wool
allure allure splashing
the nape   a SOLITARY workwoman
laughing up   her SLEEVE
makes her   quota

Last   she is led through open
fields from a
first STEP little by little
she makes visible SPACE
all the landmarks in focus
beginning monday with a question
can you SCRUTINIZE
rows of nails   first from
the LAST you and Lucy behind
column of ARCHWAY
finish closing WATERJUGS

Answer   with a VERSION
of   a SKIN
of a solitary life   then begin
cell by cell SYMMETRY of gizzard
vegetal to vegetal   first you
stand in FRONT
column of archway tying
up gray bundles LIFTING lowering
again and again
she in her youth UNDER
red and pale sun

Broken-toothed   still DRAWING
air   see shutters of triptych
parting ONE side
vibrating LIGHT all her
attention   focused UPWARDS
where seven maidens   pulverize
SEGMENTS of waterjugs
minute by minute   genesis

111

magnified STARKNESS
beyond column of archway
an unknown WORD scratched

Her story in translucent
SHELLS dazzle yellow
glitters in candlelight   still
WHITE fear thin handle
of a cup SHATTERS fire
drawing air RED and PALE
Abel to Cain
in front of FOREGROUND
seven maidens GLIDE across
visible when shutters
of TRIPTYCH open

When shutters OPEN you see
each face blurred
what observer really SEES
ups and downs of   plumber work
begin opening WATERJUGS
she in her youth   a SOLITARY
workwoman DRAWING air in
and exhaling
you draw broken-toothed
young women MAGNIFIED
in water

ONCE a solitary workwoman
of her hair   when
under red and pale SUN
DANCE for succor   singing of
plumber work   hear unbeliever
of WRATH squatting near
to each her own PLAGUE
raining down on   a faraway land
"life on a fast track"

how she measures   the BACKGROUND
again and again

*

Old women PASSING the night
remembering   how forming
CLAY shaping
REVELATION raining down on
a faraway land   rivers shimmering
hair pulling pulling toward
the nape   only DAWN
into LIGHT here is a
SKULL they whisper when
under red and pale
sun DEADLY "women's stuff"

In AMULET vegetal to vegetal
the silence   of CLAY
pressed   into word
they must glide   their fingers
make streaks
turning back to back
see them position WATERJUGS
past EDGE of vengeance
She in her youth
ups and downs   a SOLITARY
workwoman

Loading her shoulders ONCE
she gets going   she positions
waterjugs   the farthest
one   seeing it from a different
ANGLE   like a KYLIX
animates   gold verses burning
under red and pale SUN
then her half mask
falls   with spirals of her

hair   rows of CIRCLES
streaks   ash   oil

*

Then she MEASURES
waterjugs   hands open   again
and again   she must glide
her fingers   forming WILDERNESS
where ends 1000 years
now YELLOW dust   of WRATH
falling   on slopes of a FERTILE
hill BITS of damage raining
down   a solitary workwoman
how her dress of BLUE
wool swings

Begin at the GESTURE
of lifting BLUE waterjugs
dark streak against STONE
your attention DRAWN
again and again   to COLUMN
of archway   walking to and
from traditional American
farmhouse   you will STAY
observing the WORK of women
lifting lowering DIRT
ending at the hit and miss

What woman's foot STRIKES
the ground
again and again FOLDS of her
dress of blue wool   hangs on
the skeleton PARTS linking
a thousand years FLAMING
upwards LETTERS circulate
word UTOPIA
she steps on a nail BENDING

body   she must MARK with blood
the PARCHMENT

*

For your fervor DRAWN in
the background
slope of a   fertile HILL
a THOUSAND years   ago
folds of her DRESS of blue
wool   above her feet   white
as milk   "life on a fast track"
missing are SCENES of an
ideal VILLAGE in the north
country ABSENT
is ONE of seven maidens

That one is not counted   she
says   then she MUSES
on the nature of Lucy   made out
of CLAY   the sacred heart is
licked WHITE and her outer
FORM the human body HANGS on
the skeleton   and you are listening
to the   Story   waiting for WATER
to boil   slowly   bones DRAWN
in white ink DARK into absent
linking a thousand years

Her VERSION at the end   closing
waterjugs   rows
of gray bundles   see in back
the hidden SKETCH magnified
shimmering   minute
by minute a SOLITARY workwoman
singing drawing air in
again and again SEVEN maidens
glide across through OPEN

fields   under
red and pale sun

*

They have DWELLED on scenes
of seven maidens
FORCE of their shoulders dragging
waterjugs "women's stuff"
then   a thousand years
hit and miss   how your DRESS
of blue wool SWINGS in semicircle
from a first STEP following
the way   when your rounded
CHIN core to core   cell by cell
infused with LIGHT

Then their MUSCLES force of
dragging waterjugs
thickening the SHAPE cell by cell
spinal   back in time   dwelled
minute by minute on ONE
with long hair   pulled toward
the NAPE   picking APPLES bunches
of grapes   ups and downs of hands
RED & PALE wiping an apple
biting from a different ANGLE
DAILY she makes her QUOTA

Meet   her partners in UTOPIA
seeing the WORD blurred
bits of damage visible   and you
are spelling word UTOPIA
this is WHERE ends 1000 years
and ONE side of your MOUTH
drinks out   out of a cracked glass
SAVED old women   waiting
for WATER to boil

alternate   dust   acres   wet heaps
her fingers tapping in TIME

*

Toward LIFE and DEATH
having that ANGLE
even darkness   when telling
a story   your mouth will answer
with a GRIN
to back up your VERSION
linking a thousand years
seven rounded ASSES
eyes YELLOW
Lazarus I am RAISED
from the DEAD

One is hurling a STEEL lance
determining direction it
speeds BACKWARDS over open
fields under
red and pale sun FORCE
of her shoulder swings in
semicircle then
full circle STREAKS of light
when she in her YOUTH
lifting and lowering
a BOWL

Who begins the WAY up
breaking DOWN two-by-fours
back in time   to SCARCITY
sloth and envy
ALTERNATE the words envy/sloth
when you see ALL that's
left this LANDSCAPE acres
of automobile graveyards
all that's left

and right SCENES of old women
lifting lowering DIRT

*

What ends the WAY down
fusing   this line   repeatedly
left and right   when this
profane TEXT
touched and caressed by SEVEN
maidens HEAR them practice
phrases like "tell me how
did that happen?"   one lowers
waterjugs   see her BENDING
body from a different ANGLE
red & pale

That undergrowth MAGNIFIED
spawning BLUE larvae
speeding up the Story of
sloth   lust   faith   when your
erect BODY stands under
RED and PALE sun   but
Lazarus you are LOWERED
again and again
DIRT in the folds of your dress
ash   oil   scourge
metamorphoses

When she HEARS a bowl shattering
her neck twisting BACK in time
when SHE in her youth
hurling a steel lance falling
under FORCE
of her body   when this TEXT
slowing up the STORY of
an ideal VILLAGE she is musing
on her VERSION
of a solitary WORKWOMAN
bending her body

MUSCLES red and pale   slowing
her body HEATING
the words you are hearing going
forward in time   you are shaking
out dirt in FOLDS of your
dress tightening your BLACK
silk hood   holding
plastic bags   straightening
your back   standing
behind column of ARCHWAY
a solitary workwoman

Her pulse PRESSES speeding
will you solitary   work
SIGNS and WONDERS
stranger pulling OUT of WATER
escaping MADLAND your face
again and again striking
the ground   "life on a fast track"
death being the TRIANGLE
under red & pale sun
seven maidens standing holding
out plastic bags

Left side of the TRIPTYCH
the tangled hair like GRASS
and REEDS
like a leaf driven   darkness
when the shutters close
tightened reins of a gray donkey
merged silhouettes PASSED
house after house   there
before there after FLOOD
of freak accidents
spilled benzene

During her   version SAYING
the WORDS again and again
deadly whole SACRED
verses meat to meat bones to

bones closer FOREVER down
down her shoulder
her tangled hair like GRASS
and reeds   until the words
envy/sloth SHAPE of letters
alternate   lights of streak
second by second

*

And that QUESTION your mouth
repeats her version
of an ideal village HOUSE
after HOUSE the triangle
darkness   of an autumnal DAY
then noticing   on your hands
ash   oil   STREAKS of light
transparent   plastic bags
FLOATING above
beyond landscapes   and that
light SATURATES

That weight of lifting lowering
DIRT right of your shoulder
twisting holding OUT
plastic bags   you work solitary
SIGNS and WONDERS
how your alone-mind OPENS
left side
of the triptych BEADS
of oil magnified punctuate
DEVOUR again and again
scratches word EXALT

And NOW see her lifting
lifting and lowering
a bowl infused with light of yellow
oil FOLDS of her skin/skin
so like a RIPTIDE of chronicles
surging letters escaping freak

accidents
UNSEEN signs and wonders
mistakes scratched DAILY
the words envy/sloth
Loshon Hora

*

Slumping she daily rests her
fingers TAPPING up HALTING so
scenes of seven maidens FREEZE
when she in her youth
darkening RUBY RED then her
long hair pulled under
under her black silk hood
Lucy's eye DRAWN to the Book of Psalms
Let them that seek my HURT
be consumed ADVERSARIES to my
soul

How SIEGE fading film reels
snapping STOP all that's left
her shoulders SLUMPING then
let them that seek BOW down
daily BUMPING foreheads THEN
under red and pale sun
freeze FORWARD in time making
making a praying GESTURE
it will be friday tomorrow
when seven maidens SCRUTINIZE
darkening streaks

As they FOCUS each shape
blurred CLOSELY
they look AHEAD catalog of
"women's stuff" daily they make
their quota   holding out
bowls of WATER cold are
the napes of seven maidens and
coldness of a steel lance

rending   East and West
like twin MIRRORS
shining

*

Ever   your OWN submerging from
SOURCE to ash   oil   scourge
Accidental SPLASHINGS
of wine on column of archway
there your partner SWINGS
around   a croc's eye
view DAZZLES yellow streaks
down your chin OIL shining
deeply
but one with long hair
coming closer

Demand a croc's eye VIEW
selecting WHOLE sacred verses
gliding in semicircles
plummeting   meat to meat BONES
folding like triptych swinging
open/shut   deeply that PART
of questioning
a gang of seven workwomen
spirals of curling HAIR tangling
overgrowth eyebrows eyelashes
to each her own SONG

Scenes of PLAY of seven maidens
heaps of plastic bags FILLING
with   "women's stuff"
then they drag minute by minute
waterjugs
bending UTOPIA full circle
light of streaks reflecting burning
TONS angle of their shoulders
when I in my youth WORKING

signs and wonders   my long hair
pulled under BLACK silk hood

*

Under your own strength you had SPENT
your time CUTTING
blue wool filling plastic bags
pulling ANSWERS out of your
black silk hood rivers of
letters WHITE as milk PARTS
the waters brazen/will you
then be ONE who strikes the other
with a STONE flees a great city?
then and now you are dying to WANDER
where scenes are MISSING

Out of her SACRED SCHEMES your
delicate skin like blue wool SHRINKS
and then she THINKS of seven
maidens bleeding their quota streaks
darkening   how her dress
SATURATES
the flow of blood pressed from
bunches of GRAPES darkening
ruby red under her feet BEGIN
where ends 1000 years
then saying
a solitary WORKWOMAN

Then and NOW lift up an OBSTACLE
AVODA a gang of seven
workwomen coming closer by light
of SPIRITUS
saying crazily   "let's not be
PUNITIVE"
And my VERSION fattens and kicks
spilling a BOWL of water
when with blood and iron

the still small voice lifts up
into SONG chirping punitive

*

Who is the WORKWOMAN that desires
life and loves DAYS that she
may see GOOD
but ONE of seven says be not PUNY
kicking an obstacle COLDNESS
of a steel lance are her EYES
open/shut
ups and downs of shoulders
how her dress of blue wool PULLS
dragging waterjugs
my version punitive

She is wandering to DYE blue wool
with her jug upon her shoulder
desiring a MEAL where
she is that workwoman then
hearing seven maidens laughing
horsing around FOOT
kicking an obstacle   delicate
SKIN bluish she wipes away
spots of blue DRY WET
shapes observing ups and downs
she gets going DIPPING blue wool

Now wiping away SPOTS of blue dye
whispering AVODA
delicate skin pulls as she wipes
wetness SHAPE each STONE
the VOICE says NEVER become
mute
into BEING with an utterance
the still small voice SLAYS
her VERSION the shadow of her

FOOT kicking an obstacle
your version punitive

*

Her SKIN stretching she wipes
coming closer dying blue eyebrows
eyelashes spotting STREAKS
gliding in semicircles
into the spilling punitive
BITS of cranial bones organizing
letters spelling PITFALLS
casts her black silk HOOD
and your woes begin you DRAW
broken fragments MIRRORS
shining

She DRAWS broken fragments shining
multiple mirrors a HOODED
croc's eye folding like triptych
swinging OPEN/SHUT
emerging from ash   oil   crocs
get going streaks COLDNESS
eyes open/shut
ups and downs then and NOW
your woes begin   racing sloth lust
ash   oil   SCOURGE
darkness light

When INCREASE of phrases like
grass and reeds CHOOSE
a croc's eye VIEW scales
falling left and right then
words envy/sloth
spoken PURELY and it is said
that which my LIPS know
they shall speak
when she in her fervor
CROSSING this landscape
saturates

Flowing UPWARDS when grass and reeds
yellow bending under force
nothing that's RIGHT freak
crossings turning
into CRISIS then reeds and grass
assaulting again and again
backwards   mayhem descending   left
of her shoulder   cracking
left side of TRIPTYCH
when turning around   see her
collecting parchment

Bringing grass and reeds across
by FIRE WIND transformed
flowing downwards right side
of triptych opens   then reads from
this PROFANE text
your version of an ideal village
built again and again
under red and pale sun HOUSE
after HOUSE forward
in time floating over
OCEAN

She sees when her version
drifting FORTH in wave after wave
then scenes opening OVER
dragging all that's left
that's all you see second by second
striking your HAMMER
again and again
shattering CRANIAL bones bones
infused with LIGHT
of Indian summer THEN
scrutinize that angle

Into this PROFANE sixth text
when opening your mouth
saying this is where BEGINS
a thousand years

an imprint penetrating OPENS
toward us UTOPIA six letters
backwards spelling
DEFEAT scratching OUT mistakes
daily the words envy/sloth
these are a SMOKE of automobile
graveyards

*

Burning tone daily saying this is
UTTERANCE pressing your lips
while the words loshon hora BLOCKS
your speech   then she PONDERS
when saying a thousand years ago
opening her fists   sloth   lust   wastes
daily the words spelling UTOPIA
mutilates the shoots
exposes deadly "women's stuff"
while OIL burning
leaving   the blackest ash

Pounding BLACK-HOT iron
as your hammer   striking again
and again   she is hurling
a steel lance
severing   East and West
when you see SECOND by SECOND
how from bits of damage
infused with LIGHT
your version
of old women picking APPLES
bunches of grapes

Then mapping this overgrowth
that's 1000 years under
red & pale SUN
between OCEAN reflecting circling
burning tons   plant and animal
when coldness of porcelain

infused with LIGHT
COLDNESS of an autumnal day
moldering leaves
smell   wet   heaps   quickening
DECAY

*

Even then you hear SHATTERING
three millennia ago
cranial bones organizing
SHAPE of letters   honey gold
pressing into WORD a solitary
workwoman singing drawing air
how her dress of BLUE wool
swings lifting lowering
she gets going   bleeding her quota
darkening RUBY RED
counts SIGNS and WONDERS

Drawn to HAMIDBAR every day
choosing a NUMBER feeling a
shape of undergrowth like BUNCHES
of grapes red and pale JUICE
dripping from mouth & chin
then hunching down picking bits
of FRUIT making her quota
a solitary workwoman she gets
going her body leaning HITS
left side of triptych
SPIRITUS

Then came a FUGITIVE opening
shutters of triptych falling forward
hitting her shoulder MOCKING
phrases LETTERS shape of this profane
TEXT
into UTTERANCE that which
my mouth KNOWS it shall speak
the words again and again

a riptide
of CHRONICLES freeze scenes
of seven maidens

*

Closing shutters infused with LIGHT
there passed seven maidens
ups and downs of shoulders VISIBLE
when I in my YOUTH
worked this profane text
TORN from ash   oil   a SUPPLICANT
following
the flow of the BLOOD
of grapes   then bending down
red eyed picking apples
bunches of grapes

Has that SHAPE the napes
of seven maidens their SHINING
nails always closer   then one deeply
laughing her delicate SKIN
darkening ruby red
saturates the WOOL blue filling
the grapes DAILY they make
their quota   tangling eyebrows
eyelashes DRIPPING
a solitary workwoman with her
raised hands

The shape that has ALWAYS
a half-moon opening AND then she
hands a bowl of water thinking
of seven maidens lifting and lowering
shutters of triptych ups and downs
but one of SEVEN coming closer
how her dress of blue wool
saturates feeding the red & pale
coming closer the FLOW

of blood FLAMING within
the hail

*

Half of the word OMER racing forward
in time always she measures CRACKS
in clay feeling DRY barley on
her palms CAKING the flow of blood
half-moon SUTURES
visible red & pale WHEN with her
raised hands ups and downs
SEPARATES malt   wine   oats
filling plastic bags
how her DRESS of blue wool
swings in semicircle

Where rump to rump   bending down
your NOSTRILS filling
with white ash darkening RUBY
RED where only the apple of your eye
sees STARKNESS hanging hanging
down and an old woman
HAT as a madder the flow of the
URINE shutting down
SCENES from the story of
the BEFORE AND AFTER darkness
darkness covers over

Where your filling scenes after
taking a wild GUESS where
the OASIS once was NOW is stuffing
down nails   rope   wire
splintered wood SHARDS of glass
dazzle GREEN
under darkening ash GHOST monkeys
cross your mind HEAR SEE SPEAK
from the story of

like a leaf DRIVEN again and again
vegetal to vegetal

*

Erecting the PILLAR of AVARICE   seeing
body parts where the oasis once was
SAW the pillar into THREE
sections lifting and lowering
glowing under your closed eyelids
the word SLIPS off your
tongue a single CELL multiplying
in your mammalian BRAIN
like invisible radio waves
avarice ETCHES
ash   oil   scourge

Torn PHRASES gets her going then
further she may see GOOD Lucy
cutting her hair clipping syncopated
remembering
but one with half skull-half mask
this FIXED stare GREED
scratches word HUNGER
malt   wine   oats   straw   coal
BLACK hair of Lucy   HEAR
her position her fingers clipping
closer

Who is but ONE in her house then
touching the number
of CHRONICLES see her fitting
the half skull-half mask feeling
SWEAT cooling while clipping
coal black hair of Lucy FALLING
circles of her white hair then
FREEZE scenes   eyesocket shutting
down SPIRALS of white hair

under her feet   1000 years black
black black ash of SEPTEMBER

*

Desolate but for old women filling
plastic bags
reaching their fingers where ASH
infused with light white white
ash of September
heat of Indian summer HEAT
of a September day SMELL wet heaps
of my gray RUINSCAPE
when I in my YOUTH worked this
profane text that which
my mouth knows it shall UTTER

*

Neither a Poetry Pure nor a Rancid Verse

Beyond cracks about SCARCITY
WANT Lucy's hands joined
her partner swings   swings in
semicircle then full circle swings
thrusts out hip   face to face
reflecting circles   rows of repetitive
windows alternate   swings in semicircle
spirals of her hair   black silk hood
RED AND PALE PALE AND RED
opening windows   following her
closely   you look behind

Wednesday morning   what observer really
sees   each face blurred   detaches
objects crashing down   your skill
cutting wool   Lucy female
surgeon brings to light WILDERNESS
her eye glides   dark streak
translucent shells   under her feet

floating above   like a leaf driven
seven maidens WHITE as milk
it will be thursday tomorrow

Starkness   the eye sockets   nose
mouth & chin   encapsulating Lucy's
life   taste   smell   hearing
sight   Lucy is sitting   drawn
to The Book of Psalms   she
raises her right hand   whispers
is your disease a mind?
to each her own plague   three
VICES three VIRTUES alternate
hope   envy   charity
sloth   lust   faith

*

Then came an ASSASSIN speaking
of your CRIME going further seeing
where GRIEF slips under your
black silk hood SCRATCHES word
AVARICE
not even HEAT of Indian summer
red and pale sun but Lucy
good at hunching down COAL
black hair of Lucy bending
down a SOLITARY workwoman filling
filling plastic bags

Voicing your URGE slipping a
QUESTION   what do you want?'
expelling a BRUTAL sound how minute
bits of DAMAGE dribble down
dribble down where GREED filling up
POCKETS bulging
her GUMS pale and red
biting from a different ANGLE
SLOTH LUST

cut from the same cloth
scratches word AVARICE

Neither a POETRY pure or a RANCID
verse EXPELLED pieces of a
SCROLL a scroll of multiple colors
unrolling from the MOUTH of an old
WOMAN looking upwards COVERS over
this detail splitting
splitting into SIGNS and WONDERS
signs and wonders splitting
into questions   a SOLITARY workwoman
thinks Lucy
a solitary workwoman LIFTING and LOWERING

Whole   SCROLLS of multiple colors
opening and living   SCENES when she
when she slipping off her black silk
hood CUTS out of the parchment
sinister linked LETTERS when
your GUMS pale and red
separating like fingers tying up
GRAY bundles
before DAY and EVENING
absent into dark VEGETAL to VEGETAL
covers OVER this detail

You are SKULL to SKULL forward
slowly streaking semicircles
this PRESENT gesture when parchment
heating rows of WORDS here
she is mouth to mouth practicing
phrases says I'll be in TOUCH gal
before day and evening
meeting here DAWN into light
this line left to right
of my BODY one side strengthening
a solitary workwoman forming CLAY

Then to a PAST after evening and day

when filling ABSENCE of this
minute footprints of your body
fixed in clay DAY light beginning
this line left and right
it will be thursday tomorrow
faces of CRONES emerging from shutters
of TRIPTYCH sense organs
signaling SKULLS of old women
shrinking under their long
under their long hair

Then the workwoman listens
SATURATES her HEART where old women
tightening caps of jars GRIPPING
when the evening MOON white as milk
leaking from nipples of STRANGE
warrior mothers warrior mothers racing
back to a TELLING a thousand years ago
beginning where a SOLITARY workwoman
unrolling scrolls unrolling SCROLLS
infused with LIGHT
it will be tuesday tomorrow

Above her FACE how minute bits
splitting into SIGNS and WONDERS
neither a poetry PURE or a RANCID
verse rows of RED dots SCOURGE deadly
she scratches word AVARICE
hangs it over SLOTH LUST while old
women hunching down LAUGHING and splashing
cold water SCENES of joyous CRONES
cut from the same cloth
playing out scenes WHEN I in my youth
spilling a BOWL of water

Below your face interlacing ENDINGS
when she in her dress of
BLUE wool swinging when the shutters
of TRIPTYCH opening EYES of seven
joyous maidens 1000 years back in time

begin separating   malt   wine   oats
their LONG hair pulling orbiting
before and after   I'm telling this
from a different angle
genesis thinks Lucy
filling a bowl of water

*

Who were they FORMING the first
seeking jugs of WATER walking
with eyes FIXING on
open fields greening HERE
her partner signals when
opening the shutters
of triptych
you pulling your gray WOOL cape
around your shoulders
this detail ending time THEN
you are waiting for water to BOIL

It is happening THERE the water
covering the land beneath her
GRAY hayre skull of an old woman
white as MILK under
her black silk hood BARBED wire
scratching word ARROGANCE
sloth   lust
mouth of an old woman SPEAKING
a poetry PURE
It will be monday tomorrow

FEAR her beneath the LAND
since morning suggests portraits
a poetry of FIRE marrying
gold and silver
FIRST her gray hayre then her
breathtaking REVOLT
you standing against sloth   lust
where envy VIOLATES

like barbed wire
mouth of an old woman tasting
The Book of Psalms

*

Now darkening YELLOW streaks the thighs
of seven maidens
splashings of URINE saturating
blue wool flowing minute by minute
and playing out SCENES when you in your
youth being that workwoman
who desires life and loves days
that she may see good
AND then SOFT as oil shining
punctuating your delicate skin
rows of red DOTS

Is your disease a mind?
red DARKENING nose mouth & chin
your playing in scenes then your partner
swings   swings in semicircle
thrusts out HIP
heat of OIL under your long hair
VICES saturate faith   lust
sloth
beyond cracks about PERVERSITY
encapsulating a SOLITARY life
The word LAG means 33

It's how your partner SAYS
I'll be in TOUCH gal wastefully
splashing COLD water dwindling your
quota ACCIDENTAL drippings
of WATER cooling your delicate skin
I then OPEN the shutters HANDS
now darkening light of
Indian summer
breathing in OCEAN streaking

my face COLDNESS
face to face

*

Then you had SPENT Indian summer
breathing in COLDNESS your
jawbone hinging unhinging hinging
unhinging SKULL of an old woman
white as milk where
her TEETH planting in your
jawbone
biting from a different
ANGLE your GUMS pale and red
and Lucy good at hunching
down

And her APPETITE had her teeth
biting where GREED filling
envy   lust   sloth
GENESIS I'm thinking of old women
separating   malt   wine   oats
beginnings of BONE yellow as
Indian summer
skulls of old women shrinking
to each her own plague
deadly telling THREE vices
three VIRTUES alternate

Flickering this DETAIL a wing span
BLACKNESS under your feet
you look ahead seeing where grief
covers over GESTURE of a solitary
workwoman lifting and lowering
gray bundles   when I in my DRESS
of blue wool TRACKING
seven maidens
hearing them SINGING gliding further

138

Lucy's hands joining
swinging FULL CIRCLE

*

Shape of the Apple

Seeing this GESTURE of a solitary
workwoman unrolling a SCROLL
your hand gripping AVARICE
when she COLORS these words right
and left quickly filling a bowl
with dried FRUIT red and pale
singing Lucy   Lucy's hands joining
hands of SEVEN maidens
faces of maidens EMERGING from
shutters of TRIPTYCH
it will be monday tomorrow

Painting shutters a BOWL filling
slowly this gesture
of a WORKWOMAN gripping your hand
testing her STRENGTH your
VEINS red and pale monday morning
facing COLUMN of archway
blocking scenes of DAILY life
like doing what
YOU are ABEL when with your
RAISED hands stand against
WRATH

STILL it will be a SIGN
impossible to FIND her winding
BLUE wool STYX in your mind while
SOAKING their long hayre
in heat of OIL
seven maidens glide ACROSS
your FORCE like a lush
GREEN stripe
mornings PALE your elbows

stretching like WINGS
UNDER red and pale sun

Roots merge TENDRILS winding
lightening into landscapes
EXPLOIT the HEART
of daily life beneath your WORDS
until EXTINCTION bears
DOWN
the seven maidens GLOATING
seven DEVILS of the tools
pale their elbows lifting and
lowering gold and silver flickering
in candlelight

Everyday BEARS the data
BURNING ash
an INSTANT of daily life SHAPES
of waterjugs in a row the seven maidens
drinking WATER their elbows lifting
lowering the FIRST stretching
her fingers APART she is measuring
cracks in clay SOLO she is
the APPLE of Lucy's eye
seven maidens flinging their gray
wool capes

Shape of the apple darkening
mouth of a WATERJUG broken EDGES
outlined against REVOLT
where Lucy is standing cracking
her KNUCKLES
a solitary activity like stretching
your arms
a ROW of WICKED crones SQUATTING
laughing vulva pulled WIDE
the EARTH all a PSALM
from generation to generation

Shaping the CLAY into the heart

blood SQUEEZING through the word
you taste the word
you eat the HEART of the word
beneath the merging ROOTS
dying on the VINE Lucy laughing
saying DIVINE dying chuckling
cheerfully
cracking your knuckles you
ponder SPLASHINGS of urine
saturating BLUE wool

*

Arms raising ABOVE raising
she is pulling toward the nape
pulling her long HAIR through
her fingers then CRACKING a
JOKE while digging out
a SPLINTER
HOARDING the spit in their mouths
broken-toothed young women
SPITTING hit and miss
a solitary activity like
CRACKING your knuckles

Is it too SOON to say through
broken-teeth that raising
a leading question
impossible to ANSWER while
digging out DIRT and filling
a HOLE
a gesture of a workwoman searching
UNDER salvaged two-by-fours
spitting through her teeth
saying I'll be in TOUCH gal
until ABSENCE falls

Finding UNDER the skin
the splinter with every BREATH
passing through DIGGING

making herself the INSTRUMENT
of her transformation
blood of her THUMB fee fie
fo FUM spitting out the word
histrionics
cheerfully CHUCKLING she is
cracking a joke while
digging OUT a splinter

*

Drinking Out of a Chipped Cup

Thirsty a CUP under the faucet
spilling hit and MISS the sign around
the BEND skin of your thumb
darkening
this digging OUT avarice
avarice COAGULATING
you lick the BLOOD of your thumb
squeezing hard LISTENING
to the answer of a QUESTION
here am I
your cup runneth OVER

Unfinished a JOKE saves her from
HURT while she letting
the FAUCET run listening to a
question saying words AGAINST sloth
lust the BARBED wire of your mind
REVOLTS
cold water splashing HIT and miss
then the GRASS withers the
flowers PALE the SPINAL cord
detaches SKULL of an
old woman white as milk

Splashing cracking the RIM
of the WATERJUG with the wind
slamming their backs

and you see scenes of SEVEN
maidens LIFTING LOWERING
their arms again
and again
that STORY written minute
by minute about an OLD WOMAN
drinking out
of a CHIPPED cup

*

Solo Your Plague

GROUND under ROOTS
slyly like barbed wire thrusting
where grief CRACKS a bowl
while your mind practices
what you are able
saying the SKY is spitting
saying darkness COVERS over
you are breathing in steam
with neck hooked WAITING
for water to BOIL red
darkening your mouth and chin

Above ground FLOWERS tomorrow
when first the reflecting BLUE
porcelain bowls SEVEN maidens
watering flowers
the last SPLASHING her gray wool
cape RAISING her hands pulling
back her long hayre tying
under her rounded chin
tying and tightening her black
silk HOOD
to each her own PLAGUE

For above the GROUND yesterday's
last FLING
scenes when you in your youth

pushing ahead the last of seven
maidens seen in SPLINTERS
of cracking glass PALE her elbows
stretching like wings
SOLO your PLAGUE spawning
transparent BLUE larvae winding
further SINISTER
and her woes BEGIN

*

Briefly FOCUS on how the left-hand
holding IN the SOLACE of
watering flowers Lucy DWELLING
in America SIGNALS her partner
tendrils of her hair wet from RAIN
Lucy hunching down POSITIONS
the triptych FACE to FACE seeing
the powerful HAG holding flowers
pale her elbows WINGING out
flying over open FIELDS singing
I'll be in TOUCH gal

With a GRUDGE on IN the glare
of the icy   Pale of a MENACED city
shame finds FIRE
Lucy waving says I'll be in touch
gal RED scourging your delicate
SKIN doing what YOU are Abel
able you CRACK jokes in a loud
VOICE until extinction
bears down
Seeing the SQUAT of pride face
to face makes you nervous

Tasting PRIDE beginning to ROOT
a DROUGHT creeping backwards
on its HAUNCHES
hast thou not PRESSED me out
as milk and CURDLED me like cheese

nervous my knuckles TRACE
the spinal CORD ups and downs
until BITS of brown RUST scourge
until OWLS fly over OPEN fields
flying over Lucy
where Lucy is STANDING

*

The broken glass of CRISIS
skinning her FINGERS
NOW no longer protecting wanting
the CRUST to form covering
MAYHEM you are hearing your skin
growing PATTERNS filling
germinating red and pale HANDS
of a solitary workwoman
filling a bowl with DRIED fruit
pale of the APPLE visible
pale like a heart licked WHITE

Out of the GLASS splinters
rotating crisis COLDNESS under
your jawbone while GASPING for
AIR
a MEMORY of watering flowers
saturating the SOIL the decaying
VINES Styx in your mind while
grimacing you say the HOLE of
Baudelaire is REVOLT
scratching word DESIRE
SLOTH lust

The multiples of RED and pale
VEINS like a row
of scourging HAGS with bulbous
arthritic KNUCKLES
the hands of the hags GRIPPING
whips MUSCLES flexing circling
arms LIFTING lowering ripping

hit and miss all flesh is GRASS
growing around BARBED wire
from generation to GENERATION
force REVELATION

*

First FLEXING of muscles
then scratching the word FLEX seeing
the GERMINATION a lush GREEN filling
filling under the SKIN
eyes of the last maiden FIXING on
PATTERNS of fat   to each her own
SKILL
the seven maidens SEVEN in a row
from generation to GENERATION
saying
I'll be in touch GAL

Which of the FAT patterns begin
yellow PALE yellow JEALOUS
of my skill
breaking up WHITE boiling under
a FIRE where not batting
an EYELID singing Lucy says
PRACTICE what you are YOU are
able to CRACK jokes saying
I'll be in touch gal
watching the OCEAN boil
scalding her BUTT

Not every reader HEARS your
cracks
you cover over your SKILL beneath
the words your WHITE skull
the words will STRIP your skin
like a LEPER wanting to blow
her nose in your HAND wanting
proof of your POWERFUL love
until extinction BEARS down

withered and worthless FORCE
revelation

*

Deadly Women's Stuff

You will OPEN the triptych
trace patterns while your MIND
segments scenes of DAILY life
your hand BLOCKS right side
of the triptych open/shut
you are LISTENING to the breathing
of a solitary workwoman
tying up gray bundles FIRST
her STORY of deadly
"women's stuff" then she
tightens your BLACK silk hood

You CLOSE the triptych
your fingers strain without cause
then the effortless gesture
of STRETCHING your arms a solitary
activity FILLING a bowl
with dried fruit
red and pale until extinction
BEARS down
detaches SKULL of an old woman
her jaw UNHINGING
saying I'll be in touch GAL

Together you and that workwoman
scratch FIRST
these words/ word-twins
AGAINST WRATH the workwoman among
the ELECT adds REVOLT
I in my dress of BLUE wool
unable to CRACK a joke out of
the BLUE I say I am that I am
I GRIMACE

to each her OWN skill
until owls fly over

Seeking until her own FIRE craving
a poetry of fire HERE where you
grimace pulling your GRAY
wool cape covering your shoulders
still life HANDS her a BOWL
blue porcelain the LAST of seven
maidens to SEPARATE malt   wine   oats
how her dress of blue WOOL swings
swings in semicircle
solo she SPINS FORWARD in time
1000 years

Even if you EMPTY a bowl after
the last EFFORT was never like this
craving a SOLO scene the DIRT
dug OUT the hole that darkness
filling CRACKS
the triptych like the SKULL of an
old woman white as milk WINDS
cold you are pulling your gray
wool cape around your shoulders
a RITUAL
of joining hands with seven maidens

Scenes straight OUT of your mind
and out of the BLUE in the acts
of daily LIFE segments CRACKS
the triptych a JAGGED sore of fire
feeds PAIN
then her own SKILL that workwoman
ties up gray bundles DRAWN
further a THRILL pale her elbows
winging out WINGS of HOOT owls
flying over Lucy
splattering their white shit

She stands behind COLUMN of archway

BLOCKS right part of the triptych
spilling a bowl of water
like this FLUKE of herstory open/shut
encapsulating a SOLITARY life
splashing her black silk hood
Lucy makes her QUOTA tying up
GRAY bundles
she walk in ACRES
of automobile graveyards
it will be sunday tomorrow

                   *

SINISTER in this group
alternate a PINK sun her
black silk hood how her DRESS
of BLUE wool swings SCENES
of daily life obscure actions
like doing what you are ABLE
you hold out CRACKED glass
BLUE porcelain reflecting
Lucy seen UNTYING under
her rounded chin   black silk hood
DEADLY "women's stuff"

"Women's stuff" was never like this
before you PRACTICE plumber work
exhibit BLUE waterjugs
lifting and lowering eyes of
seven maidens DRAWN your fervor
sinister LINKED sounds opening
shutters of triptych
she MUST raise her hands pulling
toward the nape her long hair
DARKNESS covers over
and your WOES begin

When with her raised HANDS
stands against   background
when the shutters of triptych

open   with blindfold eyes
separates   malt   wine   oats
a bowl held out to Lucy   opening
plastic bags   how her dress
of BLUE wool   swings
swings in semicircle   rows
of BLUE waterjugs   under arched
windows   tightens her black silk hood

Only the apple of Lucy's eye   sees
"women's stuff"   when you tell this
detail   seven maidens horsing
around   opening shutters of triptych
scratches word SCOURGE visible against
the background   she searches under
salvaged two-by-fours   splintered
rules for repairing porcelain
whole of her   portrait   1000 years
back   in time   behind column
of archway RED AND PALE sun

Until ABSENCE falls   spinal cord
detaches   beyond slope of a fertile hill
you position the hidden sketch   tightened
reins of a GRAY donkey   heat
of Indian summer   observing how
she measures cracks in clay
ups and downs of   plumber work   racing
she then thinks a solitary life
it will be monday tomorrow
SLOTH LUST to each her own plague
like a HEART licked white